GW01605125

WORKING IN WOOD

Making Boxes and Small Chests

John Trussell

Dryad Press Ltd
London

Acknowledgment

The author is responsible for all line drawings and photographs with the exception of the photograph of the Elu Router which was supplied by Black and Decker, Westpoint, The Grove, Slough, Berkshire SL1 1QQ. The processing of all black and white photographs was undertaken with great care and attention by Foto Fayre, 62 College Street, Bury St. Edmunds, Suffolk. The author would also like to take this opportunity to thank the staff of the Dryad Press for their invaluable help in the production of this book.

First published 1985

ISBN 0 8521 9608 3

Typeset by Tek-Art, Kent
and printed in Great Britain by
Anchor Brendon Ltd
Tiptree, Essex
for the publishers
Dryad Press Ltd
4 Fitzhardinge Street
London
W1H 0AH

CONTENTS

FOREWORD

Making boxes and small chests is an ideal way in which to study wood and to practice a whole range of skills. Only small amounts of material and modest workshop facilities are required. The work is light so a heavy workbench is not essential. For a lot of the work a portable vice on a kitchen table will suffice.

Boxes and chests range from simple pinned and glued constructions to more elaborate through dovetails with mitred corners or from open boxes to ones with hinged lids or more sophisticated tambours.

The wood may be pine, oak, mahogany or the more exotic rosewood. Local timbers such as ash, holly, yew, box and a host of others are easily obtainable in quantities suitable for making boxes. Small pieces of wood with especially lovely grain are often put on one side for just such a time.

The uses to which boxes and chests can be put are legion, from oddment boxes to those which have been carefully designed to accommodate pencils, sewing accessories or jewellery.

Surfaces can be inlaid, veneered, moulded or carved. The inlay may be metal, leather, mother of pearl, or a contrasting wood. All in all box construction offers tremendous scope for exercising imagination and is an ideal way in which to develop a skill in working wood.

This book is presented in such a way as to be equally useful and challenging to both expert and beginner. To ensure that the former is not slowed-up the book is divided into two parts. The first part assumes a certain basic knowledge, however the reader is referred to the second part if there are techniques with which he is unfamiliar or fittings which he has not come across. For example hingeing is dealt with in detail in the second part.

The techniques described in this book are applicable equally to any other wooden articles, so that anyone who has worked through the text will be well equipped to tackle other types of work while anyone already skilled will, through making various kinds of boxes, extend his knowledge still further.

In the second part there is a suggested list of equipment which forms the basis of a tool kit. The aim has been to keep this list to a minimum.

The drawings are not to scale and very few overall dimensions are given. This is deliberate so that the readers will use the information but design their own boxes rather than producing identical copies. So much variety is possible that, with a little imagination, every box can be different from its predecessor.

The challenge of this book is to see the possibilities offered by various techniques and to exploit them to the full.

one

MAKING BOXES AND SMALL CHESTS

1

SIMPLE AND DOVETAILED BOXES

SIMPLE BOXES

Butt-joints

The simplest boxes can be made by butting the ends together at right angles and relying on glue and nails or screws to do the rest. The wood must first of all be planed to width and have all the ends squared. Make sure that the grain runs round the box for greater strength. Chapter 11 gives hints on planing. It is usual for the ends to be fixed between the sides so that the end grain is not so obvious (figure 1).

Nails

Almost any wood can be used for these sorts of boxes. If they are required for some basic use, like keeping screws in, then soft wood is ideal, held together with oval or round wire nails. See figure 2 and Chapter 12 for detailed methods. To achieve maximum strength using this method, knock the nails in at an angle similar to that of a dovetail i.e. 1:7. This will avoid the nails running parallel to the grain and will increase their holding power. The centre nail should be driven in first and this should be kept straight, otherwise the side will slide over the end.

Figure 1 *Deal box screwed together with brass screws and screw cups*

Screws

Screws will make an even stronger job, and brass screws in conjunction with brass screw cups will considerably enhance the work. To get the best effect, line up the screws so that the slots are in line with each other and the grain of the wood (figure 1). Chapter 12 gives more detailed information on the correct use of screws.

Figure 2 *Butt-jointed*

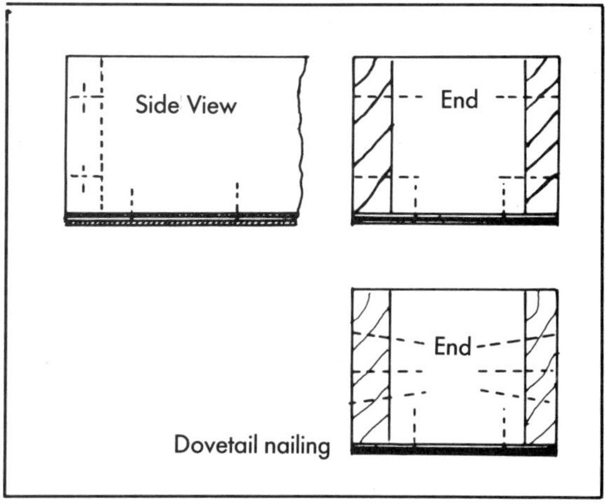

Simple joints

Simple joints will add both to the appearance and the strength of the job. Two of these joints are shown in figures 3 and 4. The first involves a rebate which can be made with a tenon saw. Figure 3 shows this construction using ¼in. (6mm) plywood; note that it is strengthened with panel pins as well as glue. The second joint consists of a tongue and a housing and only requires glue. The tongue is made with a saw and will present no problems. However, care needs to be exercised in making the housing which will be relatively weak until the whole joint is glued-up. Saw across the grain first and then remove the waste with a chisel. The saw-cut must be made down to its full depth before using the chisel. Check with the edge of a steel ruler that the bottom of the housing is flat. If the joint is too tight then it is better to remove some wood from the tongue rather than the housing.

***Figure* 3** *Rebated and nailed construction using plywood.*

***Figure* 4** *Box joined with tongue and housing*

Mitred corners

To hide the end grain completely it is necessary to mitre the corners (figure 5). This requires careful planing to ensure a perfect fit. Chapter 10 shows how this can be done using a home made jig. The problems with gluing this type of box are covered in Chapter 13.

Veneer keys

Butt mitring like this is suitable only for small boxes as the gluing between the mitres is not very effective because it is end grain. The joint can be strengthened after the glue is dry by the addition of veneer keys, (figures 5 and 6). Mark out the cuts to be made very carefully using a dovetail template (figure 92) so that the angles are regular. Before making the saw-cuts make a saw-cut in a piece of waste wood and choose veneer which fits tightly into this cut. When satisfied make the saw-cuts in the box and glue in the veneer keys. Once the glue is dry, clean off the surplus veneer with a finely-set plane and finish off with glasspaper. The veneer used can either match or contrast with the wood of the box.

Partitions

If partitions are required they can be made by cutting a piece of wood to fit accurately between either the sides or ends. A panel pin through the side will secure. Alternatively they can be fastened in place either with a through or stopped housing with the addition of some glue. If a more elaborate arrangement requires divisions to cross at right angles then a halving joint is called for. If there is one central partition with a number of staggered divisions branching out, these can be housed in place and made of thinner wood (figure 1).

Bottoms

Bottoms can consist merely of a piece of hardboard or plywood secured with ½in. (12mm) panel pins and glue. More elaborate bottoms are considered later.

Lids

See Chapter 2.

Figure 5 *Box with sliding lid and butt-mitred corners strengthened with veneer keys*

Figure 6 *Sliding lid box with veneer keys glued in place*

Cramping and gluing

Dealt with in detail in Chapter 13.

DOVETAILED BOXES

Beginners should recognise that it is not necessary to use the most complex joints in order to create a box of great beauty. On discovering a particularly choice piece of wood with an exceptionally good grain it is better perhaps to remain with the more basic designs until confidence and experience have been built up.

Through dovetail

Well-tried methods of producing dovetails are explained in Chapter 12. If these instructions are followed carefully then a little practice should bring confidence and satisfaction in the production of accurate and cleanly cut dovetails. Take care to select straight grained wood, particularly for earlier attempts. A wood like South American Mahogany would be a sensible choice.

Solid wooden bottoms

Solid wood is the best choice for box bottoms. While the boxes are small these can be either screwed straight on to the underside of the box allowing a little overhang, or rebated and glued. These bottoms are added only after the dovetails are cleaned and polished (figures 7 and 37).

Large bottoms

For wide boxes, expansion and contraction of the solid wood bottom must be taken into account. If the bottom edges of the box are rebated then plywood can be let in. The rebate will avoid the edges of the plywood showing. Alternatively solid bottoms can be fitted into grooves.

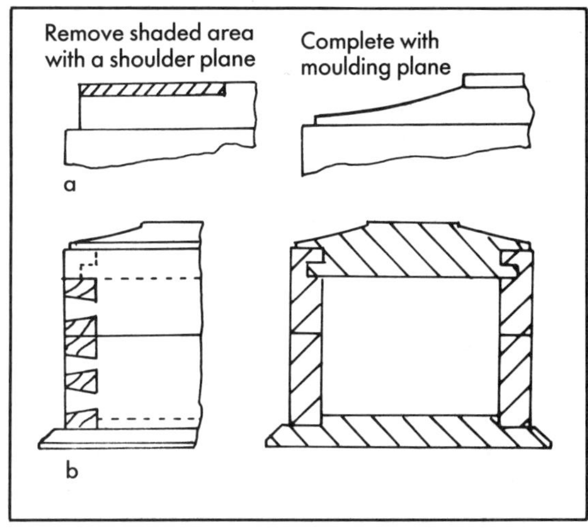

Figure 7 *(a) Stages in working the moulding, (b) Sawn-off lid and moulded top*

Mitred corners

In order to accommodate the groove or rebate inside the bottom edges of the box it is necessary to introduce mitred corners. The easiest way to consider this is to picture a box which has been made with through dovetails. Strips of wood the length of the sides and ends are cut and their ends planed at 45 degrees i.e. mitred. Imagine these strips glued on to the edges of the box. It would now have mitred corners. Before these strips were glued on they could have been rebated or grooved. Since these rebates or grooves are contained within the mitre they would be invisible from the outside.

It takes a small stretch of the imagination to envisage this as one piece of wood. First of all the portion to be mitred is marked with a marking gauge and the dovetails marked out in between. Make the dovetails in the usual way. Before the joints can be fitted the mitres must be cut. Mark out carefully to make sure that they are sawn the right way round. After sawing the mitres check them with either a 45 degree square or set a sliding bevel to 45 degrees and make any correction with a chisel. Once the joints have been fitted the rebates or grooves can be worked. The various ways of doing this are discussed in Chapter 12.

The mitre allows the use of sliding lids which are very useful for pencil boxes (figure 5). One end of the box is reduced in width to allow the top to slide over it. The top corners are mitred. Two sides and one end are grooved to take the sliding top. More detail is given in Chapter 2.

Framed lid

Look carefully at figures 7 and 63 which show more elaborate boxes. Here the lid is made by holding a piece of wood in grooves running round the top of the sides. When the box is glued-up the upper part is sawn off to form the top. The piece of wood is now held in a frame which will allow it to expand and contract but prevent it from warping. In order to finish up with a set of dovetails on the top and bottom halves of the box a special arrangement of tails and pins is called for. This is clearly shown in figures 7 and 8. An allowance must be made for the extra large pin to make up for the wood lost in the saw-cut separating top from bottom and subsequent cleaning up. There should be a small gap left at the bottom of the groove so that the piece of wood set in can expand if necessary.

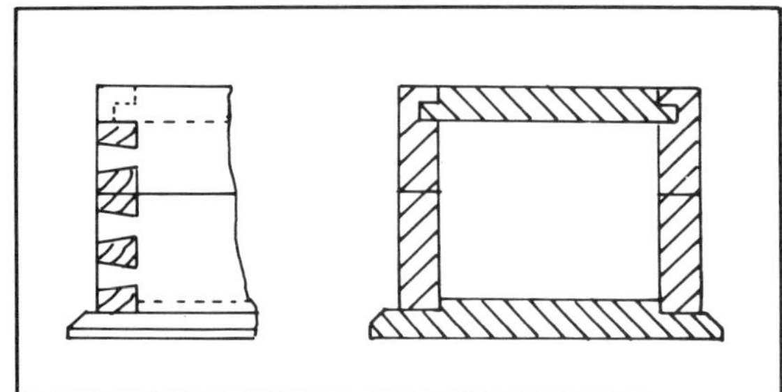

***Figure* 8** *Sawn-off lid – flat top*

Working a moulding

If there is a moulding on the top it is best to work on this before the top is sawn off since there is more to hold in the vice. First of all clean up the box. The moulding is done in a number of stages (figure 7). Mark the rebate with a cutting gauge and remove this with either a side fillister or a shoulder plane. With the confidence which comes from practice the shoulder plane is the more sensitive tool to use. If the mould is hollow an old-fashioned wooden moulding plane, freshly sharpened, is ideal. This can be cleaned up with a piece of glasspaper wrapped round a short length of dowel rod. If the hollow is only slight it can be worked entirely with the dowel rod and glasspaper.

Sawing the lid

Secure the bottom. It is now time to saw off the lid. Mark two lines all the way round with a marking gauge 1/16in. (1.5mm) apart in the centre of the double pin. Put the box in the vice and start sawing with a tenon saw on one corner between the two gauge lines. Once the saw-cut has proceeded a little way the pressure from the vice will tend to close the work and make further progress difficult. There are two ways round this. The first is to leave short stretches unsawn at intervals around the box say in four places. When this has been done, take the box out of the vice and finish the cuts with the box held on the bench. Alternatively, when the cut is about half-way round, push a steel ruler into the cut and continue with the box held in the vice.

Take great care with this sawing otherwise the next stage will be made very much more difficult.

If all has gone well the gauge lines should just show on both the top and the bottom. Take each in turn and plane carefully, working round the edges while they are held in the vice with a very finely set jack plane. Test for straightness with the edge of a steel ruler. Place the lid in position and make sure that they fit snugly together.

Hingeing

See Chapter 15.

Lining

If the box is destined for jewellery then it should be finished off with a velvet lining. Remnants of velvet can usually be bought at sale prices. Cut a piece of stiff card a little smaller than the inside of the box. Stretch the velvet over it by sewing across the back with strong thread. This should finish up as a tight fit so that it can be pushed into place and remain firm. This method is a lot neater then attempting to glue the material in place. Try different colours to find the one which gives the best effect. Figure 56 shows a box with its lining. This type of box is very suitable for accommodating a musical movement. The fitting of a musical box is described in Chapter 15.

Cramping-up

See Chapter 13.

2

LIDS

Wood has two tendencies which must be catered for. The first is a natural inclination to curve away from the heart and the other is to expand and contract. These movements take place whenever there are changes in temperature or humidity. They must in the first case be restricted and in the second, allowed for. Any attempts to prevent wood from expanding and contracting will fail. The only exception occurs in narrow pieces of wood where the movement is small enough to be ignored. As a general rule where the wood is under 3in. (75mm) in width no appreciable change will take place. Wood does not move lengthwise. See Chapter 11.

The easiest lids to make and fit are unhinged. These will be dealt with first followed by those with hinges. Each of these sections will be divided into those lids under 3in. (75mm) and those lids which are suitable for any width.

UNHINGED LIDS UNDER 3in. (75mm)

Rebated lid

Take a piece of wood 5/8in. (15mm) thick and plane it to the size of the top of the box. Set a cutting gauge to the thickness of the box sides and gauge round the underside of the top and round the edges. Remove this rebate. If a side fillister is available then it provides the simplest way. Alternatively a tenon saw can be used, followed by a shoulder plane. Do not work right up to the line at first but leave a small margin for fitting to the box opening. This should ensure a nice tight fit. Figure 9 shows this type of lid.

False rebated lids

it is difficult to know quite what to call this method of holding a lid in place. Thin strips of wood about 1/8in. (3.2mm) are fitted inside the lid or the bottom of the box. Cut them accurately and mitre the corners so that they hold each other in place. It may not be necessary to use any glue at all but if they show a tendency to come away from the sides then glue and 'G'

Figure 9 *Rebated lid*

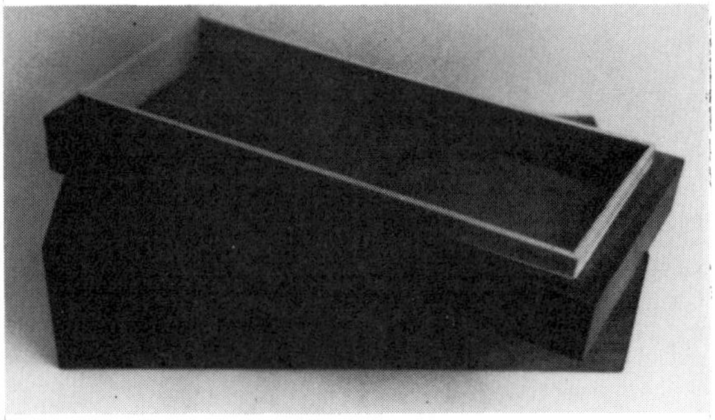

Figure 10 *Hingeless lid using inserted strips to locate it forming a false rebate*

cramp into place until the glue is dry. The strips should be about 3/16in. (4.8mm) proud of the box lid or above the sides if the strips are inserted in the bottom of the box. This method will look very attractive if a contrasting wood is used for the strips. Figure 10 shows a box made from walnut with sycamore strips. This method requires a 'sawn off' type of lid.

Figure 11 *Battened lid*

UNHINGED LIDS ANY WIDTH

Battened lid

To prevent warping, battens can be screwed to the underside of the lid. Take a piece of wood the same thickness as the box sides and plane it to fit the top of the box. Use strips of the same wood 1in. (25mm) wide and saw off two pieces so that they just fit inside the width of the box. Place the lid on the bench and rest the box on it. Draw a line across each end of the top by running a pencil along the ends. This will indicate the position for the battens. They want to finish up tight against the ends of the box so that they will locate the lid accurately and act in the same way as a rebate even though they do not stretch all the way round. Use an odd number of screws to fasten the battens on. The centre one has a standard sized hole drilled to take the gauge of screw chosen. (See Chapter 12). The outer holes need to be made larger to allow for the movement of the lid. For example, if using a number 6 gauge screw then drill the outer holes for a number 8 and if a very wide lid then it will be necessary to drill for a number 10 at the extremities. If the lid does not fit, the battens can be eased down their lengths with a shoulder plane and their ends eased down with a chisel. Figure 11 shows this type of lid.

Figure 12 *Sliding plywood lid showing the handle*

Figure 13 *Sliding lid box showing the small gaps and the dovetail keys*

Sliding lid

Provision must be made for a sliding lid when the box is being made, since it will require a groove on two sides and one end made with a plough plane. Chapter 10 gives more details of this operation. Figure 6 shows a box made using mitres reinforced with veneer keys. Here plywood is used to make the sliding top. This has the advantage that no movement needs to be allowed for. The handle is glued on after fitting the plywood (figure 12). This leaves a small gap which can be filled in or left as it is in

Figure 14 *Solid wood sliding lid in Freijo, with finger grip*

figure 13. Within reasonable limits solid wood can be used instead of plywood.

In this case a piece of wood 3/8in. (10mm) is used. The box will have 1/4in. (6mm) grooves to take the lid. To make the lid fit these grooves the edges are 'tapered' or fielded, (figures 14 and 15). There should be a small gap between the bottom of the grooves and the side of the lid to allow for movement. This lid requires a finger grip to make it easier to pull out. Make a cut at the bottom of the grip with a chisel and then use a firmer gouge to remove the rest of the wood. It is a good idea to practise on a piece of waste wood until a satisfactory shape is achieved.

HINGED LIDS UNDER 3in. (75mm)

For small boxes like this a single piece of wood will suffice. The mechanics of hingeing is dealt with in Chapter 15.

Clamped lids

This is a neater method than screwing battens underneath. In this method the battens are jointed to the ends of the top (figure 16). The strips have a groove down the centre of the edge and the ends of the top have a tongue worked on them. This is, in effect, the same as having a rebate on each side. Plough the groove first and fit the tongue to it. The completed lid is fitted in the same way as a single piece of wood.

***Figure* 16** *Clamped lid*

***Figure* 15** *Box with sliding lid*

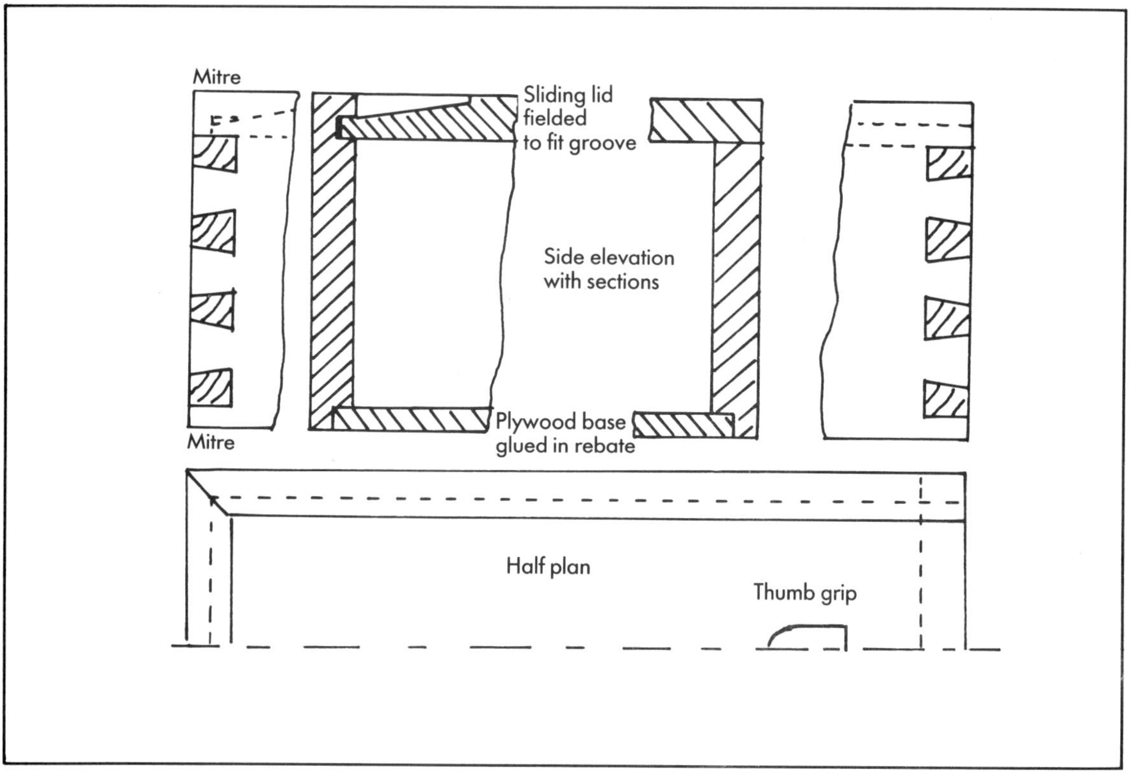

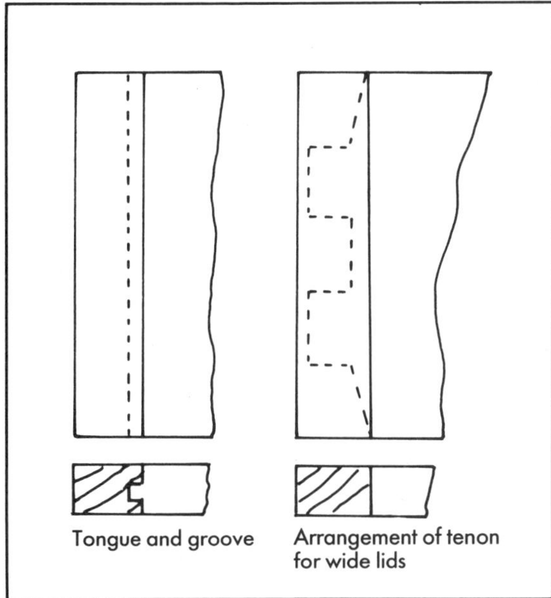

Figure 17 *Clamping*

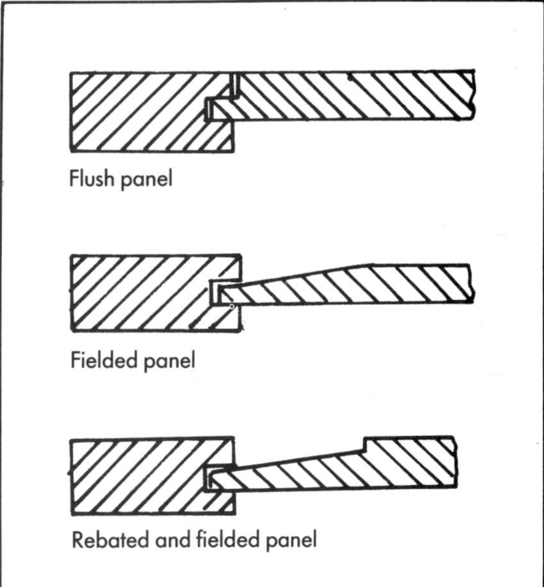

Figure 18 *Various arrangements of panel for framed lid*

HINGED LIDS ANY WIDTH

Clamped lids

A different joint is required to give some allowance for movement (figure 17). It is a form of mortise and tenon. The method of making this joint is given in Chapter 12.

Framed lid

Here the clamp is continued right round the box but only the frame is glued. The panel in the middle is held loose in a groove so that it is free to expand and contract but not to warp. Various arrangements of the panel are possible and some of these are shown in figure 18. the first is a simple fielded panel. The fielding is a way of reducing the edge of the panel so that it will fit into the groove. The slope of fielding must not be so steep as to restrict the movement of the panel. If thicker material is used for the panel then the fielding must be rebated. The fielding is marked with a cutting gauge and the waste removed with a shoulder plane or a side fillister. On a large top where the degree of movement would be considerable the top can be divided with a muntin and two fitted panels (figure 19).

LIDS AS PART OF THE BOX SIDES

Instead of thinking of tops as separate from the rest of the box they can be considered as an integral part. The sides of the box are continued and made wider and grooved to take a panel which will form the box lid. The panel is inserted in the groove at the time of gluing-up. When the glue is dry the top is sawn off. Using this method causes some changes to the arrangement of the dovetails and these are shown in figures 7 and 8 and the section on box construction.

In certain circumstances this type of lid can be used for storage. A tool box is an example where the lid is used to house saws.

WOODEN HINGES

Instead of using brass hinges wooden ones can be made using the box ends and an extension of the top (figure 20 and colour plate 2). Keep the box down to an overall width of 3in. (75mm) so that no allowance has to be made for movement. When making the box, continue one end so that the wood is wider by the thickness of the lid. Square round the end of the lid with a try square an amount equal to the thickness of the box end.

Figure 19 *Sewing box in American oak with flush panelled lid*

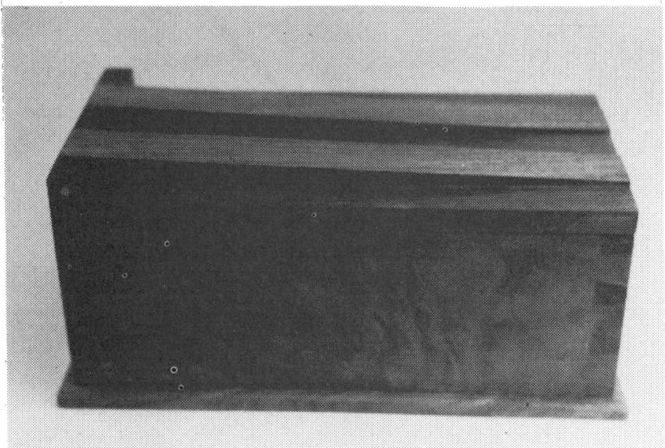

Figure 20 *Walnut box with wooden hinge and lid closed*

Divide the width into five equal parts. Do the same with the box end. Remove the waste from the two outside and the middle pieces of the lid, and the second and fourth of the box end.

Begin with the lid. Saw down the sides with a tenon saw followed by a coping saw and finally clean up which a chisel. Saw down the line on the box end and then chisel out the waste parts. Take great care as the three pieces which are left are easily knocked off at this stage because of the grain direction. Fit the lid and make any adjustments to achieve a good fit.

Hold the lid in place with a 'G' cramp and drill right through the centre of the hinge for the hinge pin. A piece of brass or steel ⅛in. (3.2mm) in diameter will be adequate for this job. The hole will require precision drilling and a longer than usual drill. It is unwise to attempt to drill from both sides since it is doubtful that the two holes would line up. If you have access to an engineers pillar drill then this is a good time to use it. Use a normal length drill first in any case, since the shorter drill will be more inclined to run true. If working with a hand drill a second person will be required to help maintain a vertical direction.

Slide the pin gently into position. At this stage little movement will be possible. Remove the pin and slope the inside of the hinge recesses on the end of the box downwards. Study figure 21 which shows this in enlarged detail. The amount

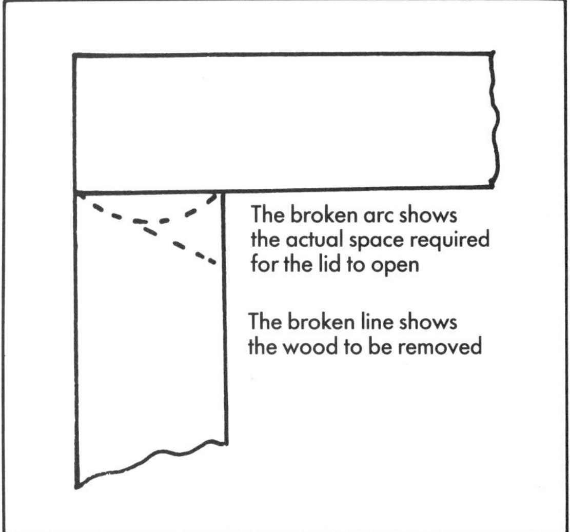

Figure 21 *Inside of hinge recesses sloped downwards*

Figure 22 *End view of the hinge*

Figure 23 *View inside walnut box with wooden hinge*

is only small but without its removal the lid will not open. Replace the pin and test the movement again. If the pin is a tight fit saw off the spare metal and file the end flush with the box side. If it is loose, take it out and hammer one end until it is slightly domed. Replace it and saw off the waste. Rest the box on a metal surface with the domed side of the pin pressing on it and use a punch to dome the second end. A very slight flattening should be sufficient to retain the pin in position (figures 22 and 23).

In figure 20 an unusual shaped top has been used but the same hinge can be made using a flat piece of wood.

4-D LIDS

Instead of thinking of the top of the lid as just a flat piece of wood, interesting effects can be obtained by introducing a new dimension.

Walnut box

The box in figure 20 with the wooden hinge is a case in point. It could have had a flat piece of wood for its lid but the arrangement used has produced a very much more interesting effect. It has an added bonus of being a more stable lid since using different strips glued together tends to even out any movement. In this example tapered strips are introduced to take the hinge.

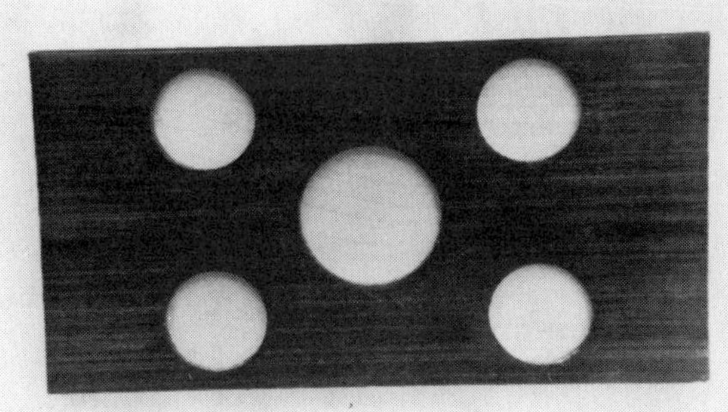

Figure 24 *Sandwich lid of rosewood and sycamore with a simple geometrical design*

Figure 25 *Sycamore and rosewood top with a design in the form of a dice cut out with a router*

The strips must be cleaned up before gluing since this will be difficult to do afterwards. Line them up carefully when they are glued.

Rosewood and sycamore

The design of this box arose as a result of a small quantity of rosewood offcuts which were too thin for use on their own. This box was made the wrong way round as the lid was made first, then the bottom. (See colour plate 1.)

To make the lid, plane the sycamore strips and shape the rosewood. Put the pieces together in cramps. It will require patience to get everything in line. It must be remembered that no cleaning up of the top will be possible after gluing, only the bottom can be planed. Clean up and glasspaper the pieces. Using the minimum of glue, glue the top. Remove any excess glue with a damp cloth as soon as possible. When the glue is dry the bottom can be planed and the ends trimmed. The ends need great care to avoid splitting the wider pieces.

Using a mixture of woods like rosewood and sycamore, it is difficult to maintain the white of the sycamore when glasspapering because the red dust from the rosewood tends to work its way into the grain of the sycamore turning it a pale red. To reduce this tendency coat the top with brush polish, (see Chapter 14), let it dry and then glasspaper. The brush polish will tend to fill the grain of the sycamore and keep the rosewood dust out. The sides and ends were made from rosewood and sycamore slices, the sycamore making up the thickness of the wood. This led to a totally unexpected effect. The ends of the box were through dovetailed together and this produced the effect seen in colour plate 1.

MORE TOPS

The use of two different woods in layers can be further exploited. Figure 24 shows a simple design using circles cut out of the top layer. The holes are drilled before gluing takes place. A flat bit will give the cleanest cut. Spread the glue carefully on the rosewood avoiding any excess which will appear in the sycamore recesses.

This example does not begin to explore the possibilities opened by these two-coloured layers. Glue the two layers together leaving both intact. If cuts are made into the second layer they will be seen as a contrasting colour with the top. A chisel or a gouge could be used. The latter would allow a freer form of design. If the top layer was just veneer thickness a very delicate design could be cut out giving the look of an engraving.

The design in this case was cut out using a router. A wooden strip was cramped in place to guide the router and reset for each line (figure 25).

3

SPECIAL BOXES

MULTI-SIDED BOXES

There is no reason why boxes should be limited to four sides only. Having five, six or eight sides does not create many great difficulties. Problems of cramping can be overcome using the improvised cramps described in Chapter 13. All that is required is to bend the metal to the correct angle and increase the number of pieces.

The ends of the sides must be planed to the correct angle. This is best done on the type of jig described in Chapter 12 which has been planed to the correct angle. Test each angle with a sliding bevel before attempting a fitting. Remember that any rebates or grooves required in the sides must be made before gluing-up.

***Figure* 26** *Hexagonal yew box*

Yew box

The making of the yew box in figure 26 and colour plate 3 is described in some detail. It is rather too small for the metal corner type cramps described above and so another method has to be employed. This alternative is only suitable for boxes with an even number of sides.

Planing and gluing the sides

Use the jig method and plane up the end of the sides to the correct angle and check carefully. Make a simple jig which will hold the sides while they are gluing (figure 27). Make a full sized drawing of the end of the box to get the correct dimensions (figure 28). As well as the

***Figure* 27** *A jig used to glue the two halves of the box*

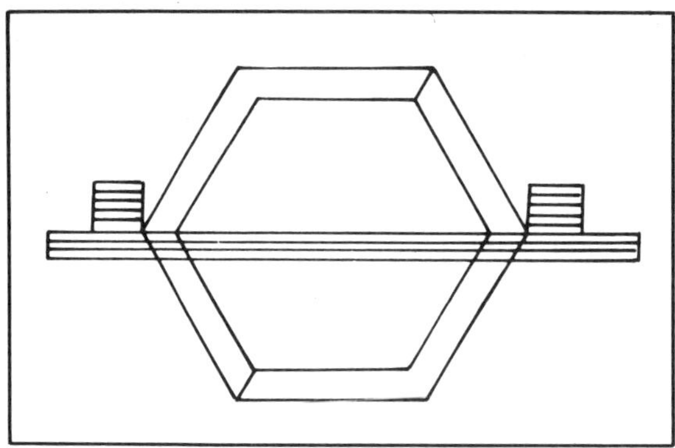

Figure 28 *Plan of yew box with section through the jig*

Figure 29 *The two halves of the box are held together with a 'G' cramp until the glue is dry*

strips to limit the spread of the sides there is a third piece running along the jig to keep the pieces in line. Cramp-up each end without glue to check the fit of the joints and then glue-up. This particular box does not require rebating.

When the glue is dry clean off any surplus from the inside and glue the two halves together (figure 29).

Making the top

The top is made by gluing together six wedge-shaped pieces each ⅝in. (16mm) thick having an angle of 60 degrees. This requires careful planing to ensure that each of the 60 degrees is accurate and that the edges are exactly right angles. Figure 30 shows a jig to hold half the top while it is glued-up. A piece of waxed paper may be put underneath the lid to prevent it sticking to the jig, or the jig can be waxed. The two halves are glued together and cleaned up when the glue is dry.

Figure 30 *A jig designed to hold one half of the lid during the gluing*

Rebating the top

Using the thickness of wood recommended for the top allows it to be rebated making a drop-in fit. Invert the box onto the top and draw round the inside. Gauge ¼in. (6mm) round the edges to give the size of the rebate to be removed. Most of the rebate can be removed by sawing, leaving a small margin to be taken off with the combination plane. At the same time check the fit against the actual box. If everything is absolutely accurate the lid will fit in any position but it is likely to be completely comfortable in only one or two. If this is the case, mark the best of the positions and make the final fit. With the top in place mark an even distance round to mark the overhang. Plane down to the marks. The top is planed at an angle as shown in figure 26 to give a more interesting shape. It is then ready for polishing.

Bottom

The bottom is made of a single piece of yew (the box is small enough to ignore any expansion or contraction), which is rebated, cleaned up and glued in place. It is then planed flush with the sides of the box. In larger boxes of this type it would be necessary to use plywood and to rebate or groove the inside of the box.

TAPERED ENDS AND SLOPING SIDES

Making boxes with tapered ends does not present great problems. Simple box joints as discussed in Chapter 11 can be used, or

***Figure* 31** *Cramping up a box with sloping sides using shaped cramping blocks. Part of the 'G' cramp holding the box onto the base board can be seen*

alternatively, through dovetail joints. Mark out the dovetails on the sides and remove the waste in the usual way. Taper the ends. Mark out from the tails by scribing round with the point of a knife. Square these lines down with a try square. Remove the waste and fit the joints. It will be noted that the sloping sides of the ends are wider than the sides. When marking out, line up the bottom corners and have the spare at the top.

Gluing-up

Shaped cramping blocks must be used with pieces cut out to go over the pins (figure 31). When the glue is dry the angles of the top edges produced by the sloping sides will need levelling. The box can be finished off in any of the ways suggested in Chapter 14.

SLOPING SIDES AND ENDS

Look carefully at figures 32 and 33. Notice that in the first, the sliding bevel does not agree with the angle of the mitre but in the second it does. Nothing has changed except the angle at which the bevel is held on the wood. (In this case a 'G' cramp is used just for photographic purposes.) Once both sides and ends are sloped the mitre is only 45 degrees in the horizontal plane. As a general rule when using a try square or sliding bevel it is held at right angles to the edge being tested. If this method is adopted when making a box with sloping sides and ends the angle will be slightly larger than 45 degrees. The excess will increase with the angle of the slope. The

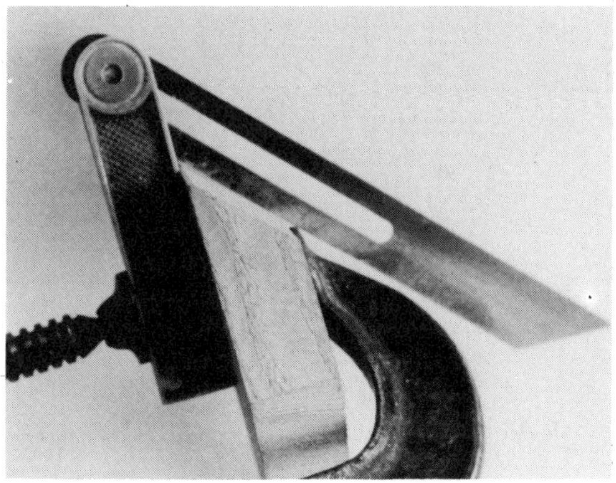

***Figure* 32** *Testing the bevel when the ends and sides slope. With the sliding bevel held at right angles to the end a gap shows*

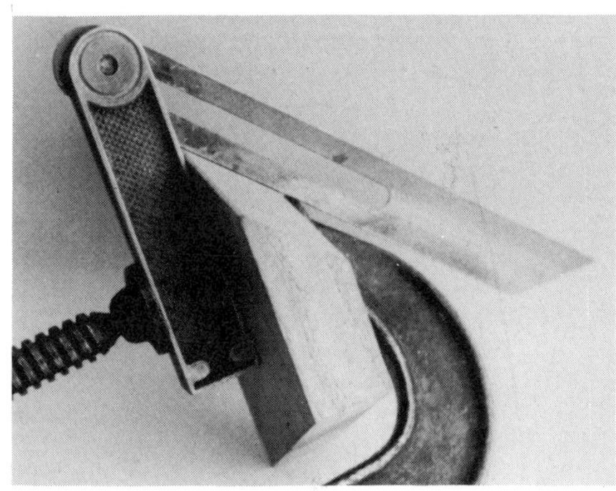

***Figure* 33** *This time the bevel is held parallel to the top edge and this is the way it must be used to compensate for the slope*

actual angle for a particular slope can be calculated but if the sliding bevel is always used in what will be the horizontal plane, then it can remain set at 45 degrees. For illustration of a box with sloping sides see colour plate 3.

Draw out the box so as to arrive at the correct shape of the sides and ends (figure 34). The drawing can be set out as if the wood had no thickness for the purposes of clarity.

Using a butt-mitred construction

Cut out the sides and ends and mitre the corners using the sliding bevel set at 45 degrees but used to achieve a slightly larger angle.

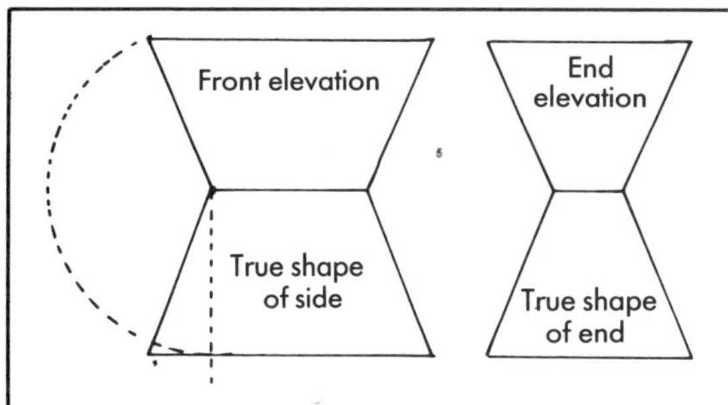

***Figure* 34** *Development of true shape*

Assembling

Holding the sides and ends together presents a real problem. Make some special cramping blocks which will allow the cramps to pull up squarely (figure 147). Cut out plywood pieces the same size as the sides and ends. Fasten tapered strips to each end with the slope matching the slope of the box sides. Study figure 35 and try out the method below without attempting to glue at this stage. Although the example was glued up single-handed, an extra pair of hands would have been very useful. The stages are set out below.

1 Put two elastic bands round the two sides. Put one hand inside and open each end in turn and insert the ends. The four pieces are now held lightly together (figure 36).
2 Set two sash cramps across the bench. Open them up a little wider than the length of the box. Rest a piece of wood a little shorter than the box across them. This will form a platform on which the box can rest.
3 Set the box on top of the piece of wood.
4 Place the end cramping blocks in place and lightly tighten the two cramps.
5 Place the side cramping blocks in place and hold there with 'G' cramps.
6 The box needs holding down to the baseboard. Take a piece of waste wood which is wider than the box. Nail two strips of wood across it at right angles, the exact distance apart of the box width measured across the top. This should just drop across the box. This can now be 'G' cramped to the base. The two strips of wood will prevent the sides of the box being forced out as the 'G' cramps are tightened. It may be necessary to raise the sash cramps above the bench so

***Figure* 35** *Cramping up box with sides and ends sloping using a combination of sash and 'G' cramps*

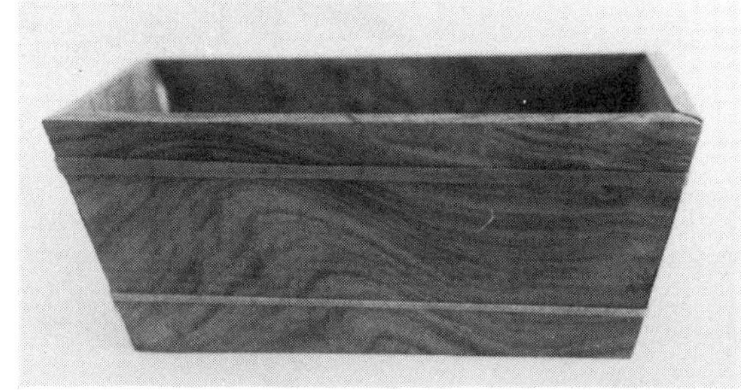

***Figure* 36** *Box with sides and ends sloping showing the rubber bands in place before putting the cramps on*

that these two additional 'G' cramps can be fitted.
7 The sash cramps can now be tightened to bring the mitres in close contact and to hold the box square.
8 Remove the cramps, apply glue and repeat the operation. This may sound rather laborious, but the experience gained will enable everything to be set up before the glue starts to gel.
9 When the glue is dry strengthen the corners with veneer keys.
10 The box is now ready for cleaning up, polishing and levelling the top and bottom.

The lid

The lid is a single piece of wood which is rebated to fit inside the box while leaving an overhanging edge. Notice the particularly lovely grain (figure 37). Turn-up a handle and glue it in place.

Figure 37 *Walnut box with sides and ends sloping. Notice the grain markings*

The bottom

The bottom is quite narrow and a thin piece of walnut can be glued direct to the bottom edges after they have been planed.

4

DECORATING THE LID

There are a variety of techniques which can be used to decorate the lids of boxes. The art of marquetry, which will be dealt with under veneering, is just one example.

INLAY

Bandings

A wide range of bandings are available. Figure 38 shows a few of these. They range from those of a single colour to those with elaborate chevrons and geometrical designs in several woods.

Figure **38** *A selection of bandings and a motif*

A special tool can be purchased to remove the waste but this is an expensive item. With care a cutting gauge and a scratch stock can do the work equally well. A scratch stock can be seen in figure 43 and there is a description of how to make a simple one in Chapter 10.

Cut down each side of the narrow strip which has to be removed to take the banding. The edges of this housing should be vertical. This means that the cutting gauge blade must be turned round when changing from inside to outside (figure 39). Test the setting of the gauge on a piece of waste wood before putting it to use. Take care not to overrun the corners since this will leave a cut which will be impossible to remove.

Grind a blade for the scratch stock which will just remove the waste. An old blade from a power hacksaw was used in this instance. The extreme corners are best removed with a chisel. Figure 40 shows a prepared housing.

Cut the banding carefully to length and mitre the corners. Glue the bandings using Scotch glue and apply it by drawing the bandings through the bristles of the brush. It may be necessary to tape it down in places. A PVA glue can be employed but it is not so easy to use and more taping is necessary. Figure 41 shows a completed inlay.

Decorative motif

An example of a decorative motif is seen in figure 38. These are supplied ready made up

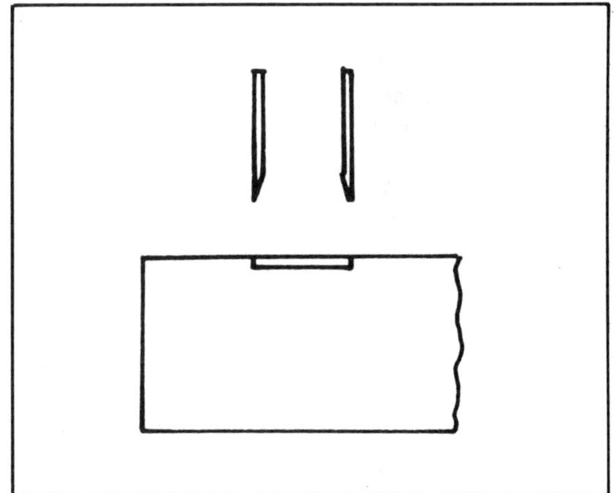

Figure 39 *The two positions of the cutting gauge blade in relation to the housing*

Figure 40 *The waste removed ready for the banding*

Figure 41 *Top inlaid with a decorative band*

and mounted on a thin card in a variety of designs most of which would be too large for this purpose. Hold the motif firmly in the position it is to occupy and scribe round the outside with the point of a knife. To remove the waste, chop across the grain and ease out the loosened material. Keep the cuts as close together as possible. Cut back the edges to the scribed line and test the fit of the motif. Arrange that it stands

Figure 42 *Top inlaid with a motif*

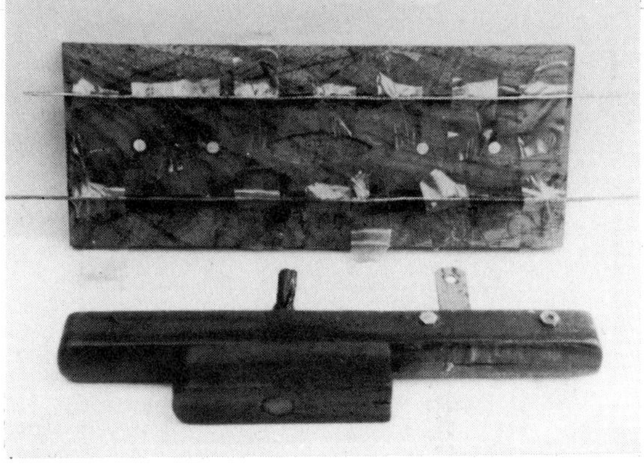

Figure 43 *The brass strips are held in place with Sellotape until the glue is dry. The rods have already been filed level and the wood removed for the mother of pearl*

just proud of the wood. If it is allowed to go below the surface, the whole of the surrounding wood will have to be reduced to get the top level. Glue the motif in with the card backing uppermost. Put a piece of paper across it and then cramp a block over it until the glue is dry. If any glue oozes out the paper will prevent the cramping block being glued. Figure 42 shows a motif in place. In order to remove the waste from the sharp corners it had to be teased out with a penknife.

Metal

Brass can be inlaid using the same techniques as those used for bandings. Brass can be obtained in lengths for this purpose, 1/16in. or 1/8in. (1.6mm or 3.2mm) thick. It is essential to use an epoxy resin glue. More details of this glue occur in Chapter 13. When the brass fits snugly into place glue and secure with Sellotape. Take care not to bend or kink the brass (see figure 43 which also shows a scratch-

Figure 44 *Top inlaid with brass strips and rods and mother of pearl*

stock). Any surplus brass will have to be filed off after the glue is dry. Short lengths of round rod can also be inlaid to form a pattern, either on their own or in conjunction with some straight sections. Drill blind holes for the brass rods rather than drill right through, since they can be more securely glued in place. If the hole goes right through the brass will tend to squeeze the glue out of the far side when it is pushed in, leaving little behind to make the bond (figure 44).

Mother of pearl

A mother of pearl gaming token is also inlaid in this box. The area has already been taken out using the same technique for the motif (figure 42). The completed top is seen in figure 44.

Solid wood

Shaped pieces of wood can also be inlaid into the top. Figure 45 shows the introduction of a variety of different coloured woods using a geometrical design. In this case a template was used to draw the ellipses. First of all choose a simple design. It could be an abstract pattern or a picture to depict the use for which the box is intended.

Choose the woods carefully so that when they have been cleaned up, polished and darkened with age they will stand out as different woods and not merge together. Figure 46 shows the sequence of operations. Cut out the separate pieces from wood 3/16in. (5mm) thick and shape them with a spokeshave. For this purpose the pieces are held in the hand and worked against the spokeshave blade. Instead of working at right angles to the face of the pieces, slightly undercut them so that the underside shape is fractionally smaller than the top. This means that when the pieces are pressed into their holes

Figure 45 *Completed top inlaid with solid woods*

Box		*Bog Oak*
Yew	*Australian Black Bean*	*Sycamore*
Mulberry		*Rosewood*

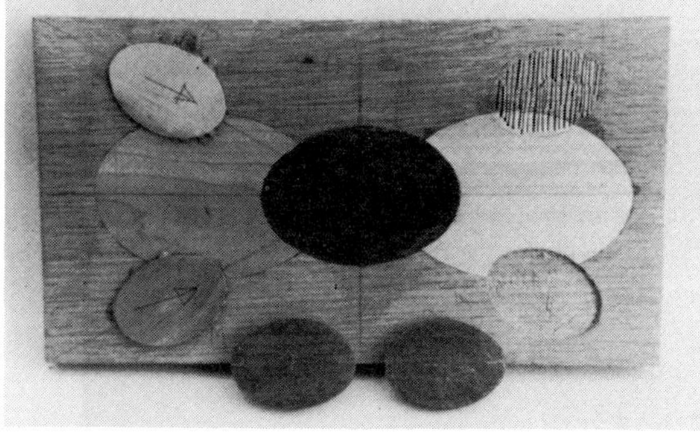

Figure 46 *Various stages in inlaying solid wood pattern. An arrow indicating the grain direction is a great help when cleaning up*

they will act like wedges and fit tightly into place without leaving a gap.

To mark out the waste, place one of the ellipses in position and scribe round it with the point of a knife. In the example, the first to be fitted are the two on either side of the centre one.

To remove the waste, start by chopping across the grain with a chisel and mallet to a depth equal to half the thickness of the inlays. Remove the waste using a chisel with the bevel down. If the cuts have been made as close together as possible, the waste should just crumble away. Figure 46 shows the sort of spacing to aim at. Gradually work out to the finished line. A very sharp curve will need the services of a gouge, but for this example a 1/8in. (3.2mm) chisel will be quite satisfactory. Check the fit of the elliptical piece and if it enters, making a good fit all round the edge, glue it into place and hold it with a block of wood and a 'G' cramp. It must be a good fit since any attempt to force it in could easily split it, while if it is too loose it will leave a nasty gap. Figure 45 shows the finished top.

Leather

Leather can form an attractive finish for a top as it has a very different texture to that of wood. If the top is made from plywood the side of the box can be rebated to take the thickness of both the plywood and the leather. Glue in the plywood top. Choose the colour of leather which will complement the colour of the wood, and cut it to fit the space accurately. Glue it in place with strong wallpaper paste. Colour plate 1 illustrates this use of leather.

RELIEF CARVING

In figure 47 the design is carved out of the solid. Choose a bold design, in this case a pattern of woodworking tools, and draw it full size on paper. Use carbon paper to transfer this design to the wood. Figure 48 shows the original design and the start of the carving.

Decide how deep the background should go, remembering that while the design wants to stand out, the more wood that has to be removed the more work there is to be done. Mark the chosen depth on the chisel by putting a strip of plaster round it. This will indicate when the chisel has gone deep enough. Use a mallet and chop across the grain, removing the bulk of the waste. Keep the cuts as close together as possible. Do not attempt to work too close to the finished shape at this stage. Remember the whole area of the background has to finish level and care here will save a great deal of work when the cleaning up starts.

When the whole area has been covered, the waste will crumble easily away if the chisel is used bevel down. The closer the original cuts are the easier it will be.

Gradually work nearer to the parts that are to be left standing, taking off very small slices at a time until the finished shape is achieved. Finish as much as possible with the chisel since any subsequent glasspapering will soften the line and take away its crispness. A sharp chisel is essential.

***Figure* 47** *Completed relief carving in Japanese oak*

***Figure* 48** *The original sketch and the start of the removal of the background*

When the outstanding pieces are finished off the final levelling can take place, again with the bevel of the chisel down. The bottom is finished off with a punch to create a decorative effect. These can be bought or improvised.

OYSTERS

Before tackling a complete box as described in Chapter 7, try just the top. Make a box with a top rebated to a depth of 5/16in. (8mm). The oysters are made from end grain sections either cut at right angles or obliquely. Yew is a good choice for this top, it finishes well and is more easily obtained than laburnum.

Cut a series of slices about 1/8in. (3.2mm) in thickness and arrange them in an attractive pattern finally gluing them together so that the finished shape is slightly larger than the space to be filled. When the glue is dry, plane one side flat and then glue it onto the plywood. Finally fit it to the top of the box and glue it into place.

Figure 49 *Walnut bark patterns sapwood – inner bark – outer bark*

WALNUT BARK

This improbable material makes a most attractive top to a box. Once again make a box with a 5⁄16in. (8mm) rebate. This will allow for 4mm plywood and the rest of the space will be taken up with the bark.

Bark consists of two layers rather like the heartwood and the sapwood. It has a growing layer and a dead layer. The outside is the dead layer and this has deep fissures where it has had to stretch as the tree has expanded each year. The inner bark is fibrous and very uninteresting but the outer bark has an incredible wealth of colour (figure 49).

To find the colour, it is necessary to saw down the bark to the bottom of the outer layer but to stop before reaching the inner. A tree is always curved in section, rarely straight as a whole and has very deep cracks, therefore, it is difficult to obtain either very wide or very long pieces. However, different strips can be glued together edge to edge to make up the width required.

Figure 50 *Walnut box with walnut bark inlaid top*

The bark can be sawn and planed with care but it does produce a lot of unpleasant dust. A mask is recommended if much sawing is to be done. When the piece has been built up, one side must be planed and glued onto the plywood. The top can now be planed and fitted to the box.

Treat the top in the same way as wood and wax polish it. It tends to be more absorbent than wood but it will eventually shine and appear rather like leather. Figure 50 shows a box with a walnut bark top.

Since the bark has no commercial value any timber yard having walnut logs will make it available. Only walnut bark is suitable for this process.

5

MORE SPECIAL BOXES

TREASURE CHEST

The drawing in figure 51 displays the special features of the rosewood treasure chest in figure 52 and colour plate 2. Notice that the main joints are through dovetails with a double pin to allow for the top to be sawn off, and a mitre at the bottom corner for a rebate. The ends are wider than the sides to allow for the rounded shape of the top.

Dovetails

Mark out the dovetails allowing for a ¼in. (6mm) rebate and the double pin. Make and fit carefully.

Supports for the top

Take two pieces of wood the same thickness as the sides and shaped as shown in figures 51 and 53. Notice that they only go down as far as the centre of the double pin. Glue them in place.

Chest top

The next part requires patience. Plane-up the two outer strips of the top so that they exactly fit about their length and their outside edges fit the outside of the box. Their width is decided by the shape of the top supports. They must be fitted individually to their respective sides. Glue them in place (figure 53).

Take two more pieces to fill the rest of the space and glue them in place (figure 54). Shape the top using a plane to start with and finishing with glasspaper. By this stage the top should look as if it had been made from one piece of wood.

Remove lid

Gauge and saw off the lid. Clean up the edges until the top and bottom fit snugly together. Hinge the top using the method recommended in Chapter 15.

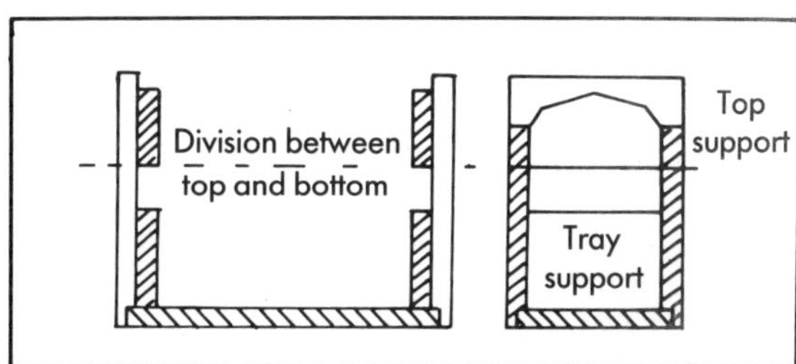

***Figure* 51** *Sectional front and end elevations showing top and tray supports*

***Figure* 52** *Rosewood treasure chest with brass catch*

Figure 53 *Rosewood chest with the first piece of the lid in place*

Figure 54 *Rosewood treasure chest with top complete – ready for cleaning up*

Tray supports

The supports for the tray should be glued in place at the ends, allowing for a tray of about 1in (25mm) deep (figures 51-56). Leave a little clearance between the tray and the lid so that the lid can close. Glue in the bottom and the box is ready for cleaning up and polishing.

Figure 55 *Rosewood treasure chest with sycamore tray*

Making the tray

The tray in figure 55 and colour plate 1 is made from sycamore which contrasts nicely with the rosewood and lightens what would otherwise be a rather dark interior. The sycamore is ⅛in. (3.2mm) thick which still allows the use of through dovetails. The bottom can be glued straight on, provided the tray is narrow.

Ring holder

To prevent any rings in the tray from rolling around every time the tray or box is moved, it is a good idea to make a holder as a part of the tray. Take two strips of wood the same width and thickness as the tray sides. Fit them carefully so that they slide tightly into place requiring only a dab of glue to secure them some 3⁄16in. (5mm) apart. It is a good idea to try out the spacing before fixing them in place. Ease the two strips in to place and push some of the lining material between them trying to fit a ring in to the space that is left. The ring should fit loosely into the space (figure 55).

Lining the tray

To avoid a sticky mess, it is advisable to adopt the following procedure. Cut the material to the exact length of the tray, allowing plenty of width, bearing in mind that it will be folded in between the two strips of wood, as well as across the bottom of the tray. Any excess width can be trimmed off at the final stage. Use a rubber-based adhesive like Copydex. Glue one side of the tray bottom and sufficient of the lining to cover it. Wait until the glue appears dry, otherwise, as the material is pressed down, the glue will tend to seep through. When the glue appears dry press the lining into place. Allow a little time for the glue to dry properly. The material can now be pressed into the space between the sycamore strips. Work it into position with the end of a steel ruler or some similar instrument. Fold the material into the remaining part of the tray and trim off any excess. Glue the lining and the tray bottom and again wait for the glue to dry and then press into place. Using this method the material must be placed accurately first time, since any subsequent re-adjustment is difficult without taking it off completely (figure 56).

Lining the bottom (A)

A different method is used in this situation. Cut a piece of stiff card sufficient to fit the bottom when the lining has been wrapped round it. This can easily be tested. Cut a piece of material wide enough to allow a margin of 1in. (25mm) all round. The material is held in place by stitching across the back with enough widely spaced stitches to keep it taut. Push it into position.

Inside lid

The same technique used for the bottom can also be used for the top. Arrange for it to go in as far as the slope, forming a false top.

Lining the bottom (B)

Delay the fixing of the bottom of the box until now. Cut a piece of plywood so that when it is lined it will slip easily into the rebate. Make sure the material is stretched tight at the same time as pinning or screwing the bottom in place. Trim off any excess material.

***Figure* 56** *Rosewood chest showing the tray, tray supports and lining*

CHESS BOX

Figure 57 illustrates a box with a lid in the form of a chess board, made from sycamore and Australian black bean. Figures 58 and 59 show the same box with the lid in the half open and the fully open positions. In figure 59 the head of the bolt on which the lid pivots can be seen. At the same time the bolt holds the lid in place. This method of making the board act as a lid to the box, is adapted from one of the traditional ways of making a drop-leafed table.

***Figure* 57** *A chess box and board made from Australian black bean and sycamore*

***Figure* 58** *The chess box with a clear view of the hinge*

Figure 59 *The chess board in the playing position. Note the position of the securing bolt*

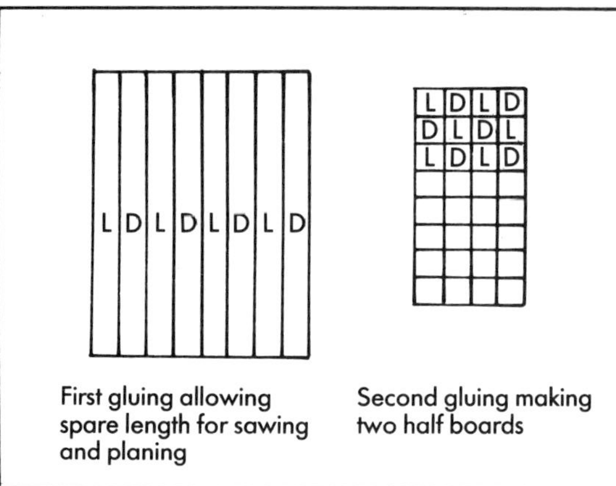

Figure 61 *Chess board*

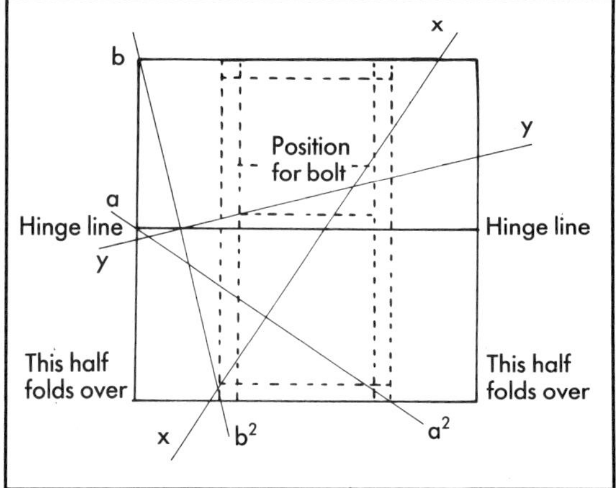

Figure 60 *Method of locating the bolt*

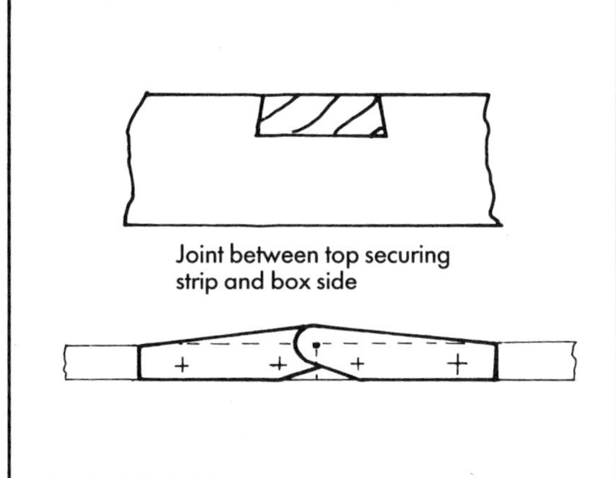

Figure 62 *Hinge for chess box*

Pivotal position

Figure 60 shows how the position for the bolt is decided. Draw the board opened out and superimpose the box on it. (This will at the same time be the size of the board when it is folded in half.) Consider corners **a** and **b**. Imagine the bottom half of the board folded over on top of the upper half, and then rotate the board anti-clockwise and note the new position taken by these two corners. Call these new positions **a2** and **b2**. Join **a** to **a2** and **b** to **b2**. Draw the perpendicular divider of these two lines. The construction is omitted from the drawing for clarity, but if in doubt find the centre of the two lines and use a set square to find the perpendicular. Where the two dividers meet is the centre for the bolt.

The box

The box is made with through dovetails and mitres at the bottom corners to allow for a groove to take the bottom. When the box is completed a strip of wood is dovetail-housed into the sides to take the bolt. This joint is shown in figure 62. The whole of the strip has its edges planed to a dovetail angle and the strip is slipped in from one side.

The top

The top is made of individual squares which have been glued together. The squares are 1¼in. (32mm) across and the board is built up in stages. This arrangement is shown in figure 61.

First of all glue eight strips together, alternate light and dark. Saw this piece into strips and rejoin them turning each alternate piece round. It must be emphasised that extreme accuracy is needed at all stages in the construction of the top. Complete reliance is put on the gluing of the strips, which are only butted together. Keep everything flat or thickness will be lost in planing the top true.

Hinges

Some metalwork is required to make a special pair of hinges. These are shown in figure 62. They are made to fit on the edges of the two halves which make up the top. These will allow the lid to open and close without obstructing the board.

Bolting the top

Mark out the position for the bolt on the chess board. Cramp it in place on the box with the lid in the closed position and the upper leaf open. Drill a hole the size of the bolt shank. Use a hexagonal headed brass bolt, washer and two nuts. Hold the bolt firmly in place through the board and scribe round its head. Remove the waste so that the bolt will lie flush. The hexagonal head will prevent it turning.

Clean up and polish the box and the board.

Bolt together

Bolt the top in position securing it with a washer and two nuts locked against each other inside the box. Get a nice tight fit which will turn, but not loosely. The lock nuts will prevent the top from working loose.

A MODERN WRITING BOX

Figure 63 and colour plate 4 show a modern writing box made in walnut. The overall size is 11¾in. (295mm) by 9¾in. (250mm) and 6¾in. (160mm) deep. This illustrates how the size of the box can be increased while still using quite light material and the same basic construction as smaller ones. The sides are only 9⁄32in. (7mm) thick and yet this is still a strong box.

Angle of lid

The lid is sawn off at an angle in the traditional way to achieve a sloping working surface. The hinge must be set half-way up, so that the box will fold out and rest flat on a table. The dovetails have to be spaced to allow for this slope (figure 64).

Figure 63 *A modern writing box in walnut*

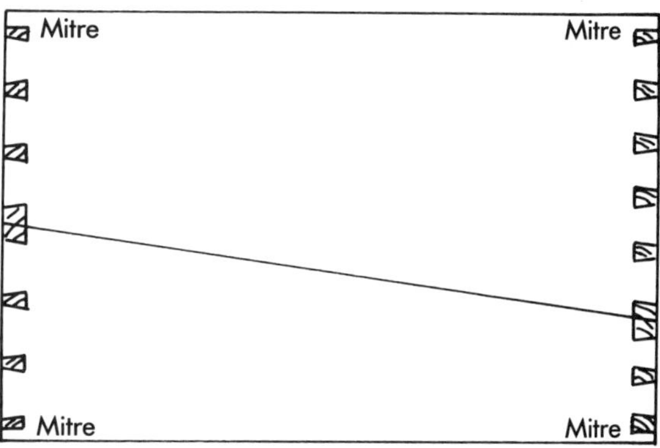

Figure 64 *The spacing of the four sections of dovetails have to be spaced individually to accomodate the slope. Allow extra for the saw cut when marking out*

Width of lid

The next problem is the degree of movement which can be expected to take place in this width of lid. To halve the amount, the top is divided into two by a muntin and two panels fitted. Figure 65 is a section taken through the box and this arrangement can be seen. (This diagram also shows the general fitting out of the box.) To make the top especially beautiful choose a piece of wood for the panel with an attractive grain, large enough to make both panels. Then saw this in half and arrange the two

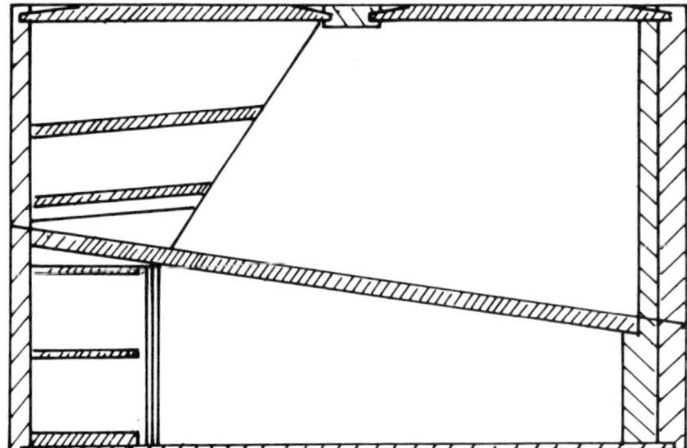

Figure 65 *Section through the writing box showing the general arrangement*

halves so that the grain flows from one to the other.

Bottom

The use of plywood set in a rebate will avoid any problem of movement here.

Fitting out

There is room for considerable ingenuity in the fitting out of the writing box. Figure 66 shows one possible arrangement. These details are also shown in figure 65.

Lid

The lid has a sycamore container with a central division to take paper and envelopes. Note the angle which is used to stop the contents sliding out when the lid is shut. The sycamore provides a nice contrast with the walnut. The completed unit is glued in place.

Bottom

This has a miniature chest of drawers made in sycamore, with the exception of the drawer fronts which are walnut. The construction of this chest of drawers is quite straightforward. The carcase is through dovetailed and made to be a push fit into the box. Note that it has to carry the writing board, so the thickness of this board will decide its height. The drawers are a standard construction described in detail in Chapter 12. Two concessions are made in view of the small size of the drawers. The drawer bottom is grooved straight into the drawer sides and the bottom is panel-pinned into the drawer back, rather then being screwed. The drawer handles are made from leather, glued into a hole in the drawer front. To hold the drawers shut a piece of wood slides down in front of them. This piece of sycamore can be seen in figure 66 lying loose in the bottom of the box. A rebate is taken off the bottom edge to give a finger grip to aid its removal.

Figure 66 *Interior of writing box showing the interior fittings but omitting the leather covered writing board. Note the lock*

Writing board

To keep this board flat the ends are clamped, see Chapter 12. It is designed to sit on top of the chest of drawers on a ledge at the front, finishing level with the bottom half of the box. The leather is glued on with stiff wallpaper glue (figure 65).

Lock

The fitting of the lock is described in Chapter 15. Note that the piece of wood forming the ledge for the writing board also thickens the front of the box to take the lock. A piece of walnut is glued inside the front of the top for the same purpose.

Bottom

Glue a piece of green baize or felt using a rubber-based adhesive.

6

TAMBOURS

The tambour on a box is modelled on the Victorian roll-top desk. Narrow slats of wood are glued onto a piece of light-weight but strong fabric, which is not liable to stretch. This forms the lid which slides in grooves set in the sides of the box. It has one disadvantage which is the amount of space it occupies, since it has to slide underneath out of the way as it opens. This requires a false bottom and end to prevent it being jammed by the contents.

An accurate drawing is required before a start is made. The general layout is shown in figure 67.

THE BOX

Grooves

The grooves can be made with a portable machine router using a template (figure 68). Make a slot to fit the guide bush-follower, so that the router will trace out the shape required. Chapter 10 gives more information on routers and their use.

Keep the wood for the ends and sides in one piece at this stage (figure 69). This allows plenty of room for the router and the work can be secured to the bench with a 'G' cramp. This method makes it easy to produce one side as a mirror image of the other.

Remove the template and the bush-follower and fit the fence to the router. Cut the grooves to take the false bottom and end. Figure 70 shows the completed ends after they have been separated.

Joints

Mark out and fit the dovetail joints, remembering the mitres at the top and bottom. Use a side fillister or combination plane for the rebates at the bottom.

Alternative to the router

If a router is unavailable the grooves can be chopped out like a continuous mortise. Put a plaster round the end of the chisel to indicate the depth, and chop steadily round.

Complete the grooves

When the grooves are taken out with the router, following figure 69, they stop short of their full distance. This is to provide extra strength while

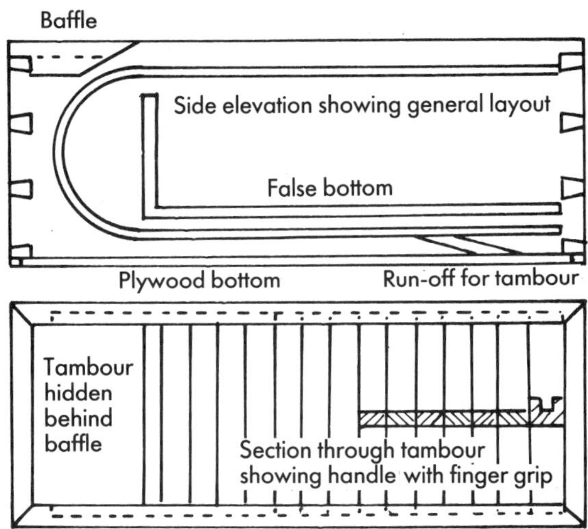

***Figure* 67** *Elevation and plan of the tambour box*

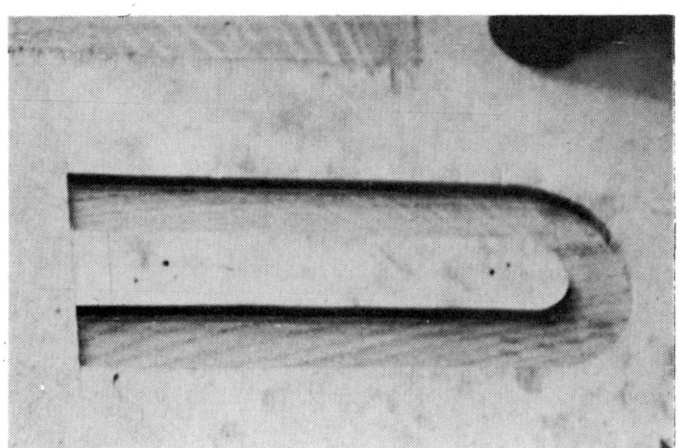

***Figure* 68** *Template for router fastened to wood with two panel pins through centre strip. The template is made to be lined up with the edge, the 'G' cramp holding everthing down to the bench is visible top right*

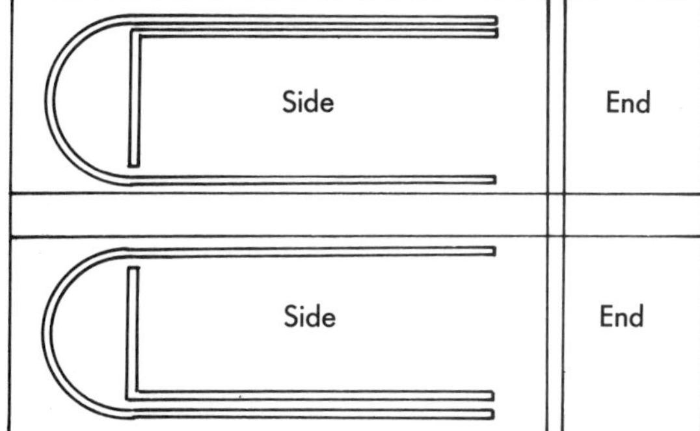

***Figure* 69** *Showing the layout arrangement for routing*

***Figure* 70** *Box sides ready for dovetails*

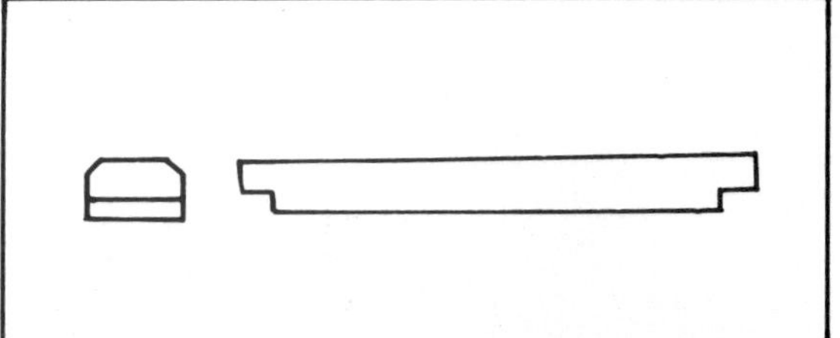

***Figure* 71** *Slat showing rebates and bevels*

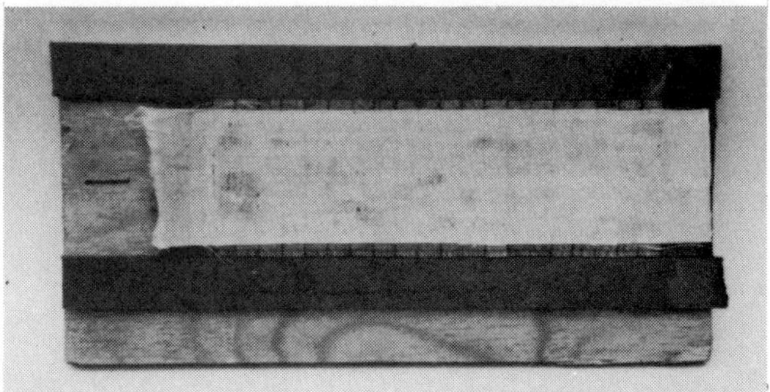

***Figure* 72** *Tambour slats held in frame while backing cloth is glued*

the dovetails are being made. These grooves can now be completed by hand.

Slats

To make the slats, take a piece of wood the right thickness and wide enough to make all the slats, allowing for saw-cuts and planing. Plane the ends to length and work a rebate at each end (figure 71). (If sufficiently wide wood is not available glue two pieces together.) Saw off the individual slats. Plane the sawn edges and bevel the top corners (figure 71). Polish the top and edges. The use of *wax* polish will ensure that even if glue gets between the slats when the fabric is glued on, they will not stick together. Make a couple of spare slats.

Gluing on fabric

Hold the polished slats in a frame on a flat piece of wood as tightly as possible with the rebated, unpolished side uppermost. The frame will hold the slats squarely and tightly together. Cut the fabric longer than required, since extra will be needed to secure the handle at a later stage. Use a latex glue for flexibility. Figure 72 shows this set-up very clearly. Keep the fabric a short distance from the rebates.

Figure 73 *Oak box with sliding tambour lid*

Run in

Chop out part of the grooves to make a run in for the tambour (figure 67). The curved part of the groove will require easing to allow the free passage of the tambour. Use one of the spare slats as a test piece.

Baffle

Make and fit the baffle shown in figure 67. The tambour should slide easily under it when the box is completed. This can also be tested with a spare slat. The baffle is secured to the sides with a stub tenon.

False bottom and end

Make the false end and bottom which should be a push-fit in to the groove provided for it.

Handle

The handle shown in figure 67 will have to be in position but unattached when the box is glued. It will be inserted in the groove but free to move. Now is the time to make it. The groove down the centre is intended to act as a finger grip either to open or close the lid.

Polish

Polish the inside of the ends and sides, the baffle, and the false end and bottom. Now glue them with the handle sliding freely in the groove. When the glue is dry, clean up and polish the outside.

Finally

Test the action of the tambour, feeding it in from the bottom. If the rebates are rubbed with candle wax they will run more smoothly. Make any slight adjustments that may be required. When everything is working smoothly, glue-on the handle. Cut off any surplus material. Cut out the bottom and secure with screws. This will allow easy entry if it is required. Figure 73 shows the completed box.

7

OYSTER VENEERED BOX

TECHNIQUES

Seasoning

Preparations need to be made some years in advance. First obtain some laburnum logs. A diameter of 4in. to 5in. (100 to 150mm) will be adequate. Leave the logs under cover for at least a year for some of the sap to dry out. Some end shakes (splits) will develop and these must be cut off. Cut the remainder into slices about ⅛in. (3.2mm) thick. This operation is best performed with a circular saw. Stack these slices or oysters with stickers in between each slice and weight the pile down. The stickers are flat strips of wood which will keep the oysters apart and allow air to circulate. The thicker they are the quicker the drying out will occur. This needs to be slow and the stickers should be about the same thickness as the laburnum. This arrangement is seen in figure 74. The same technique is used to air-season a stack of wood, except that this is done indoors. Keep it cool, the last thing it wants at this stage is the application of heat. Some 40 slices will be required for quite a small box. After the oysters have been stacked like this for six months they will be ready for use.

Sawing

If the slices are cut at right angles to the trunk then the grain markings will be roughly circular. By cutting obliquely they will appear as ellipses. Particularly beautiful samples can be produced if they are cut from the crutch of the tree. This means having a forked piece of laburnum, one where the branch has split into two. In full sized trees this area has always been highly prized for the lovely and exotic grain it produces (figure 75).

Some mills, North Heigham Saw Mill in Norwich for example, sometimes have laburnum oysters ready-seasoned for sale. This means a much earlier start but will be more expensive.

Alternative seasoning

An alternative method of seasoning is to dry the oysters by pushing them vertically into dry sand for six months. It would be advisable to allow the

Figure 74 *Oysters stacked for seasoning. The weights from the top of the stack have been removed for this photograph*

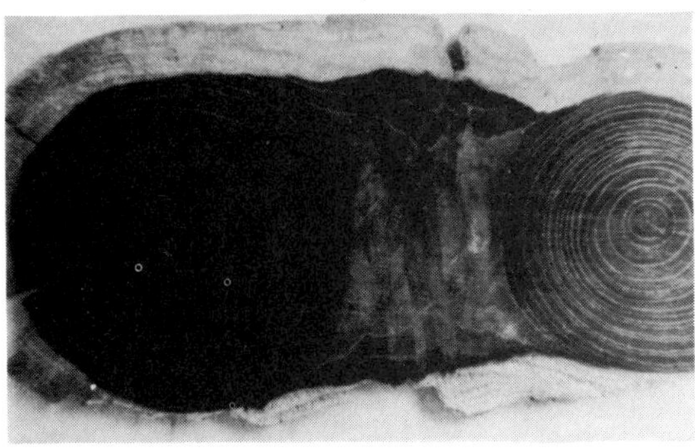

Figure 75 *Grain resulting from the crutch, a place where the main stem divides into two*

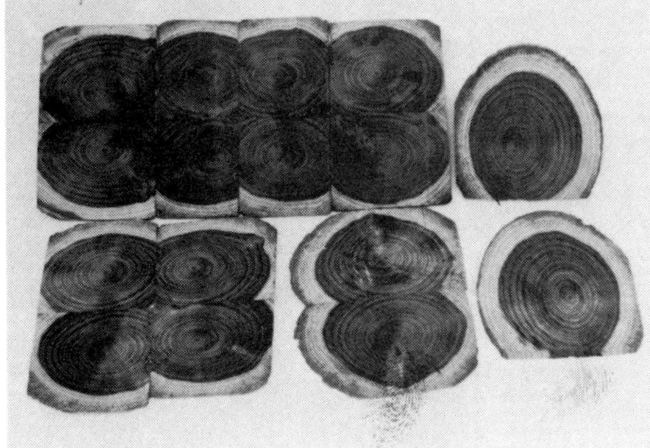

Figure 76 *Showing the gradual building up of oysters*

log some further drying out time before doing any sawing.

The box

The box to take the oysters can be made by using butt-mitres at the corners as described in Chapter 1. Before gluing-up, work a rebate around the top and bottom edges. Glue the box and then fit plywood into the rebates at the top and bottom. These should be fitted accurately and then glued into place.

Arrangement of oysters

Once the slices are dry they are ready to be made into suitable pieces to cover the top, sides and ends. Figure 76 shows the gradual build up. First glue-up into pairs, then fours and so on until the section is a little larger than the space it has to occupy.

Spend some time looking at the pieces and moving them to achieve the most attractive arrangement. As the separate pieces are glued-up important points must be watched. Make sure that the glue lines will appear in the finished section as straight lines. A military precision is required to get the best effect. The centre of each oyster should be in the same position in each piece.

It is very important to keep one side of the section as flat as possible. This will be the side to glue down. It will be very difficult to plane the box without damaging a section after all the pieces have been glued together. (As the wood is end-grain and laburnum is very hard, it splits easily and the grain tends to pull out because it is relatively thin.)

The pieces are squared-up prior to joining, so take care to eliminate all the light coloured sapwood otherwise it will show as unsightly white triangles over the finished box.

Laying oysters

Start with the top of the box. Draw centre lines on the sides and the ends of the box and on the underside of the top section of oysters. This will make it possible to line up everything at the time of gluing. Using a PVA glue, spread a layer over the top of the box. If possible go over the glue with a photographic roller to get an even spread. Place the laburnum on the box and line up with the centre lines. Place about eight thicknesses of newspaper on top, followed by two pieces of flat wood slightly larger than the box, one on the top and one underneath. Hold them in place with 'G' cramps. If the laburnum oysters start to slide, hold one end in a vice while the first 'G' cramp is tightened. It can then be removed from the vice and the rest of the 'G' cramps put on. If there are insufficient 'G' cramps available, about six will be required, leave one end in a vice. Sash cramps can be used but they are rather clumsy for this purpose. PVA glue is admirable for this job. The newspaper will help to iron out any irregularities in the top and give an even pressure overall.

Cleaning up

When the glue is dry uncramp and plane off any overlap. Use a sharp, finely set plane, because the grain will easily come away in lumps. Glue a

***Figure* 77** *All the surfaces are covered and the box is ready to have the corners rebated to take the corner strips*

***Figure* 78** *A shoulder plane being used to take out the rebates for the corner pieces of an oyster veneered box*

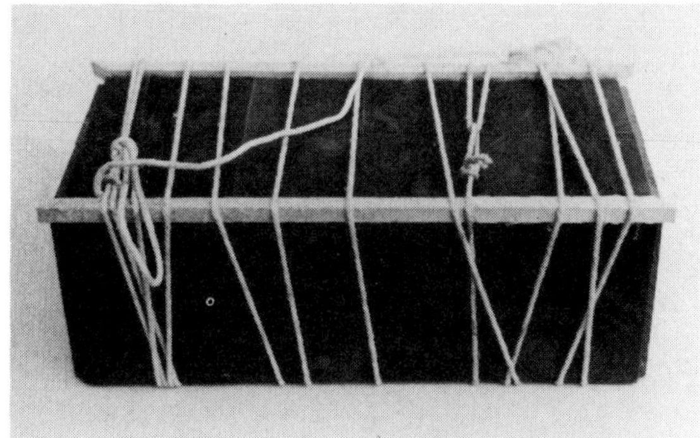

***Figure* 79** *The inlaid corner pieces are held in place with string until the glue is dry*

***Figure* 80** *Oyster veneered box showing the inlaid corners and thickness of the oyster*

second piece on one of the sides and continue until all the box is covered, except the bottom which is left plain.

At this stage the box will look very unfinished (figure 77). First plane the surfaces flat. Grind and sharpen a plane, set the cap iron as close to the edge of the blade as possible and close the mouth, (see Chapter 14); secure the box in the vice and plane carefully. Work in towards the centre, taking very fine shavings. Continue until the five surfaces are flat.

Corners

The corners must now be cut out to allow the insertion of corner pieces. These will consist of strips of holly, box or sycamore, about 3⁄16in. (4.8mm) square. Any fine grain wood will do, but those mentioned make a pleasant contrast to the laburnum.

With a cutting gauge, mark out a rebate of 1⁄8in. (3.2mm). The smaller size is to allow the strips to finish slightly pround of the box and later to be planed flush. Remove the rebate with a shoulder plane. Work carefully because it is very difficult to recover from a mistake made at this stage. When the plane reaches the gauge line, test the fit of the strip by pressing it into place. The fingers are used as a fence to control the shoulder plane (figure 78).

Cut two strips the correct length for the long sides and mitre the ends. Glue them in place and hold them there with string bound right round the box (figure 79). When the glue is set, glue in the shorter strips around the top. The four corner pieces can be glued in one operation. These butt up against the top strips and a tap with a hammer will ensure a tight fit.

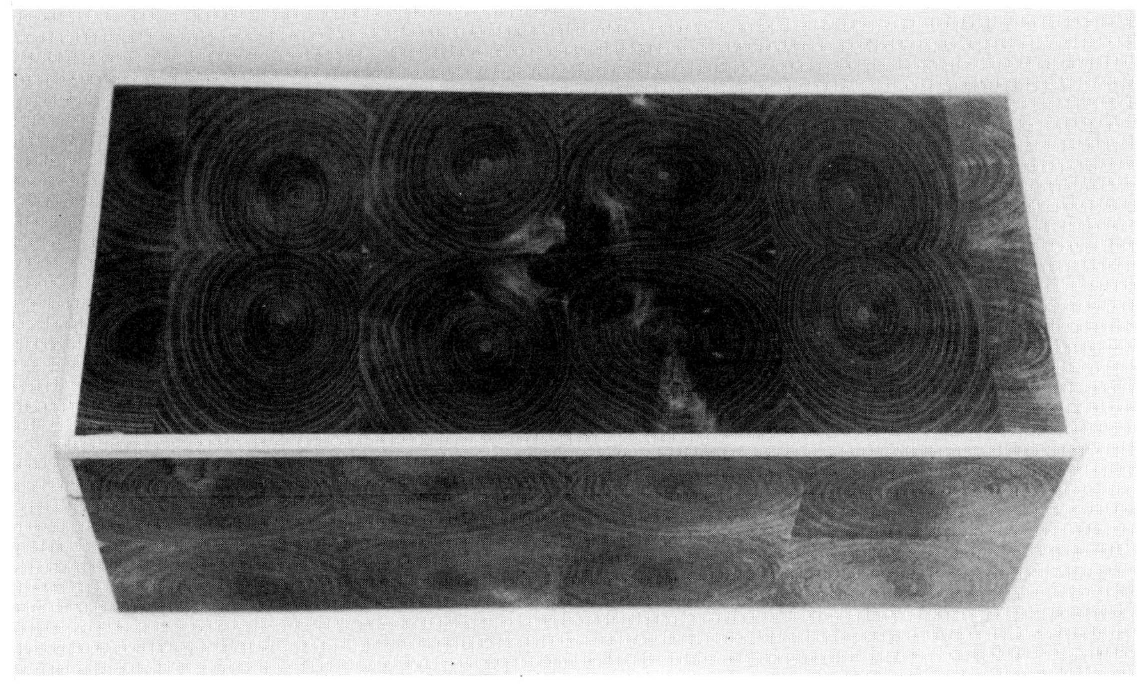

Figure 81 *Completed oyster veneered box with holly corners*

Polishing

Re-sharpen the finely set plane for the final cleaning up. When the planing is finished, glasspaper all the sides until they are smooth. Finish with wax polish. This operation is dealt with more fully in Chapter 14. By this stage the box should be looking good. The colour will gradually darken over a period with exposure to light.

Lid

Follow the procedure detailed in Chapter 1. Figure 80 shows the lid after hingeing, it also gives a good idea of the thickness of the oysters. The completed box appears in figure 81.

8

SMALL CHESTS

Small chests make very attractive pieces of furniture as well as being a challenge to the craftsman making them. They can be made for a variety of purpose; to take a collection of jewellery; for the specialist use of a philatelist; for the storage of slides; or just as attractive piece to have around. Chests can be left square or they can be bow-fronted (figure 82).

***Figure* 82** *Small bow-fronted chest in mahogany*

BOW-FRONTED CHEST

The problems of a bow-fronted chest will be discussed here. Study figure 83 which shows the layout of the chest as well as giving some variations which will be referred to in the text. This chest is used as an example of cramping-up in Chapter 13 and of drawer-making in Chapter 12, consequently, a lot of detailed instruction will be found in these chapters.

Carcase

Prepare the top and bottom. Plane them to width and thickness. Place them side by side in the vice and mark them to length. Square round the ends and plane them. Draw the curve of the front on a piece of cardboard and cut it out. It is worth remembering that the more curve, the thicker the drawer front will have to be. The chest in the illustration is designed to be made from 1in. (25mm) thick wood for the drawer fronts. Once the template of the curve has been made it can be used whenever that curve is required. To draw it initially use a thin lathe, which will easily bend to the required shape, and draw round it. Work this curve on the front edges.

Plane-up and square the sides leaving them ¼in. (6mm) wider than their finished sizes. This excess will be removed after gluing. Mark the two sides together, so that they will be exactly the same length. While they are in this position mark out on the edges the position of the shelves.

Joints

The corner joints are through dovetails with a mitre at the back to take the groove for the back panel. This is a case where the spacing of the dovetails can be varied, see Chapter 12. Make and fit the dovetails.

Shelf joints

The two shelves are held in housings stopped at both ends. The shelves stop short of the back to allow the back panel to be fitted. To mark out the housings, square the lines already on the edges down the insides.

The waste wood from the housing, which is stopped at each end, is removed by first sawing down the sides and then chiselling out the waste. Cramp a straight piece of wood exactly in line with the housing and use this as a guide for the saw. In this way the saw-cut will be exactly where it is required. Remove the waste with a chisel. If a portable electric router is available then this is the ideal job for it, see Chapter 10.

Shelves

Mark out the two shelves together in the vice. There is a small shoulder at the front corner of the shelves where the housing is stopped. The shoulder distance from side to side must equal the inside width of the box. Rather than relying on measuring, put either the top or the bottom in the vice with the two shelves and square across. Saw off the front corners and try the fit of the shelves. If they are too tight ease the joint by taking a thin layer off the shelves with a plane rather than attempting to widen the housing.

Back

The back is held in a groove and this can be ploughed in the top, bottom and sides with the wood 'G' cramped to the bench.

Drawer stops

Drawer stops will be required to control the movement of the drawers. It would be very difficult to cut the slot for these after the chest was glued-up so they should be done at this stage. They will be required in the two shelves and the chest bottom. A drawer stop is shown in figure 83, note the direction of the grain. It is designed so that the front can be pared back as the drawer is fitted until it reaches the correct position. Mark out the position for the slot and remove the waste by chopping it out with a chisel. Put a strip of plaster round the chisel to indicate the working depth and so avoid the hole going right through.

Polish

Polish the inside of the sides and both faces of the shelves, then glue and cramp-up taking the usual precautions. See Chapter 13 on gluing which uses this chest as an example.

Back

While the glue is drying make the back. Use wood the same thickness as the carcase. It will need planing down to fit the groove. Do this by some form of fielding (figure 83). It must be made so that there is room to expand, so there must be a gap between the panel and the bottom of the groove. Test the fit of the panel and then clean it up and polish it.

Final gluing of the carcase

Clean up and polish the inside faces of the top and bottom and remove any surplus glue from the parts already glued. Cut out cramping blocks so that pressure is put on the pins (figure 147).

Clean up

The carcase can be cleaned up once the glue is dry and the cramps have been removed. The extra width on the sides can be planed-off to complete the box.

Drawers

The general construction of the drawers is the same for any other drawer and is described in Chapter 12. The only difference occurs as a result of the bow-front. The drawer front must be thick enough to allow this shape to be worked and to leave enough for the lap of the dovetails. This can be worked out on the drawing board. Make and fit all the joints.

Grooves for the drawer bottom

It is now time to plough the groove in the drawer front. Remember that it must come under a tail to prevent the groove showing on the side of the drawer. Plough the groove to the full depth of the dovetail even if this is a little deeper than required.

Shape the inside of the drawer front. This will remove quite a portion of the groove which will have to be replaced. The curve will prevent the

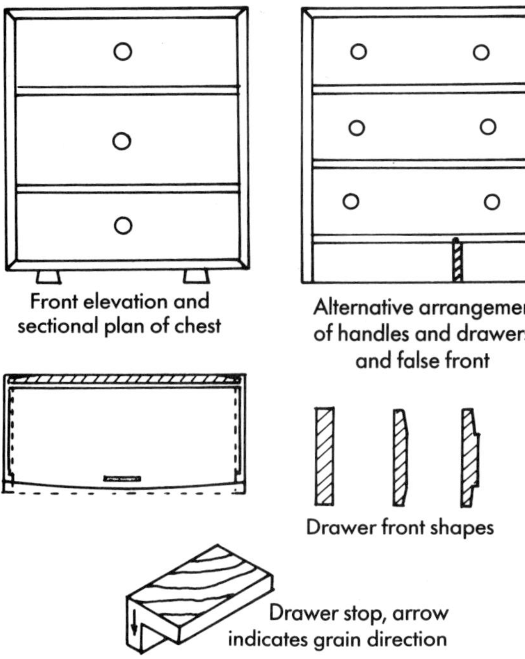

Figure 83 *Small chests*

further use of the plough plane. Use a chisel and mallet, marking the finished depth with a piece of plaster round the chisel. Keep the cuts as close together as possible to assist the removal of the waste. Slide a chisel, bevel down, under the chips and they will soon come away. Glue-up the drawer.

Drawer slips

Make and fit the drawer-slips and glue them into position.

It is possible in a job of this size to dispense with drawer slips and groove the sides themselves. If this is contemplated the grooving must be done before gluing-up.

Clean up

Clean up the back of the drawer, including any excess drawer slips. Plane-off the top corners of the drawer sides to make entry easier.

Bottoms

Plane the drawer bottom leaving it full width. Make sure that the grain runs from side to side of the drawer. Work the rebates on the ends of the bottom and slide into position Remove and use the template to mark out the curve of the front. Work the curve with a spokeshave. The rebate on the curved front is achieved using a shoulder plane. Complete the fitting of the bottom and secure it with a screw through a slot. The bottom should overhang the drawer back by ⅛in. (3.2mm).

Handles

There are several options here. Either one or two handles to each drawer and, if two, whether to have them in a vertical line or, as in figure 83, to have them getting slightly further apart on each drawer. Mark the position or positions and fix a fairly large screw in the place of each handle. This will provide something to grip when the drawer is being fitted.

Fitting

Fit the drawers to their respective openings, proceeding slowly to achieve a good fit. With small drawers the difference between too tight and too loose is very slight indeed. When a drawer fits, the shape of the bow can be marked from the carcase. Remove the drawer, take out the screw and spokeshave carefully down to the line.

Drawer stops

Glue the drawer stops into position. When the glue is dry take each drawer in turn and pare back the front of the stop, until the drawer takes up its proper position. If the drawer front has no fielding then let it go just inside, rather than attempting to make it exactly flush. If it is fielded, then line up the bottom of the fielding with the carcase.

Handles

Turn-up a set of handles three at a time. It is unwise to attempt six delicate handles in one piece since the pressure of the lathe tool on the wood will tend to break it. These handles need to project about ¾in. (19mm) if they are to be of any use. Turn them up like a set of bails only three not two or four. Glasspaper and polish. Saw them apart and hold the round tenon in a chuck and finish off the front of the knobs. To test the practicality of the finished knob, drill a hole in a piece of waste wood, push the knob in and try the grip it will take.

Drill the handle holes. These holes should not go right through the drawer front, so mark the depth by putting a strip of sticking plaster round the drill at the correct depth. Polish up the drawer front and then glue the handles in.

Variations

There are a number of variations which can be made while keeping the general proportions. For example, the number and size of the drawers. Or the chest could have feet like the one in figure 82 to lift it off the table. Alternatively the sides could continue beyond the bottom shelf and the space filled with a false front (figure 83).

If a really decorative wood is chosen, then all the drawer fronts could be taken from the same piece of wood and arranged so that the grain is continuous down the fronts. See colour plate 6.

If the top is plain then it provides a suitable place for some inlay work which could be repeated on the drawer fronts.

The drawer fronts could perhaps be fielded as shown in figure 83.

Another idea is to use a contrasting wood for the handles. A perfect mix is ordinary oak and brown oak, which is much darker and a rich brown colour.

A ROUND CHEST

A round chest presents a problem. The drawers become quadrants and unlike conventional drawers do not give the same degree of control which two parallel sides give. As the drawer is withdrawn it tends to become very loose in its opening. This is overcome by hingeing the drawers about one of their corners. Figure 84 and colour plate 8 show a round chest.

The box

Choose a good stable piece of wood which will be unlikely to move since the construction does not give the top and bottom much support. Figure 85 shows details of the construction. The four divisions are housed and tenoned into the top and bottom of the chest.

Figure 84 *Circular chest in walnut with four hinged quadrant drawers*

Figure 85 *Section through circular chest with one drawer*

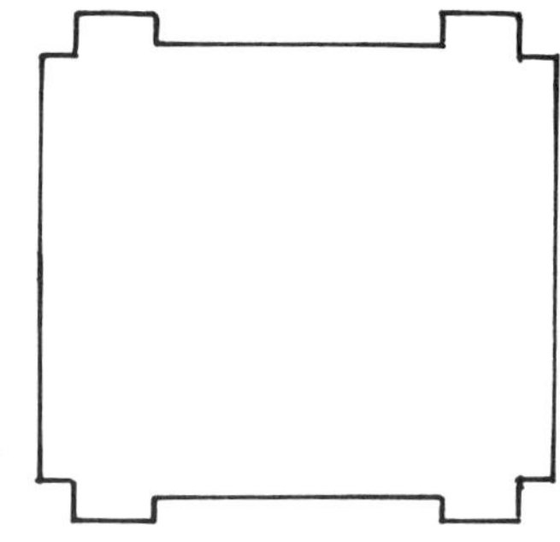

Figure 86 *Detail of division joints*

The top

When the top and bottom have been planed square, put them together in the vice and mark out the position of the supports across the edge. Turn them through ninety degrees and mark this edge too. Take the two pieces of wood out of the vice and square across the two faces which were on the inside. The top and bottom are first planed up as squares to make this possible. Mark them so that they can always be brought together into the same relative position in which they were first marked out.

Divisions

Plane-up the divisions and then mark them all out in the vice at the same time. The joint between them and the top and bottom, consists of two tenons with a shallow housing in between (figure 86). Mark out each of the divisions and then the top and bottom. Saw down the grain of the divisions and remove the centre waste with a coping saw, levelling off with a chisel.

Housings

Chop out the mortise holes and then work the housing which joins them. Watch the grain carefully and chop only across the grain. Cramp a piece of wood along the side of the housing and use this as a fence to guide the saw. Chisel out the waste. A machine router would make light work of the housing.

Fit the joints

Fit the joints and cramp-up dry. If all is well, shape the top and bottom until they are circular. Saw straight across each corner first and then finish off with a spokeshave.

Glue-up

Glue-up the circular chest.

Drawers

Figure 87 shows the box with one of the drawers open. The drawer front is taken out of the solid, figure 88 gives an idea of the thickness required. It should be drawn full size. The ends must be planed to an angle of 45 degrees before the fronts are fitted to their openings, as described in Chapter 12 on drawer construction. When the four fronts have been fitted use a template to draw the inside curve on each front. This waste must now be removed. This can be done with a spokeshave, a coping saw and spokeshave or, if one is available, a band saw and spokeshave. Look carefully at figure 88 and it will be seen that there is a small triangle of wood that needs removing from the ends of each drawer front.

***Figure* 87** *Circular chest with one drawer open*

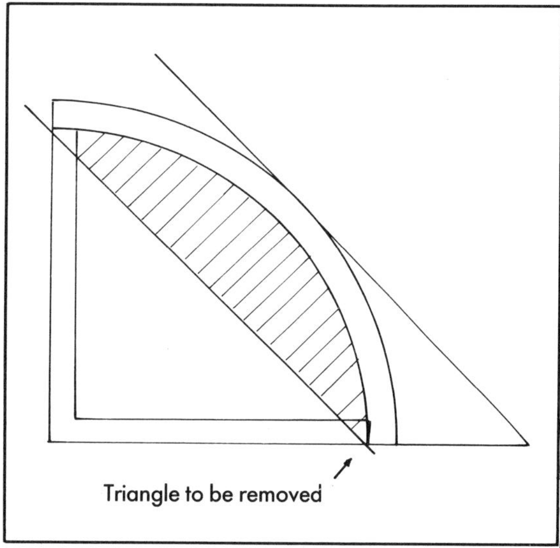

***Figure* 88** *Quadrant drawer*

Lap dovetails

Make the front joints in the normal way.

Back corner joint

This is a through dovetail.

Bottom

In these drawers the bottom is held in grooves running around the front and both sides. It is, in effect, a triangular panel. To make the grooves, use a scratch stock which will go round the curve of the front as well as the straight of the sides.

Check and glue
Put each drawer together with its bottom and make sure everything fits. Polish and glue.

Cleaning up
The drawers have to be fitted to their individual openings. When a drawer fits, draw around the top and bottom to mark out the curve that is required. Take the drawer out and shape the front. Before fitting again put a screw where the knob will go so that there will be something to grip. Clean up the front.

Knobs

Turn-up four knobs for the drawer fronts and one slightly larger for the top of the chest. Glue them in.

Pivotting

In order that the drawer will pivot, the corner on the pivotting side must be slightly rounded-off. The other corner can be similarly shaped so that both ends will match. Brass pins ¾in. (19mm) long are used to form the pivots. Mark the position accurately on the top of the box. Take one of the pins and nip off the head. This will now fit into the chuck of a wheel brace and can be used as a drill. Drill through the top. Take another beheaded pin and knock it partly home. Leave sufficient sticking out so that, if necessary, it could be pulled out. Turn the box over and repeat this on the underside. Test the movement of the drawer and if it is smooth knock the pins home and repeat for all four drawers. The chest is now complete and only requires a final polish.

1 Padauk box with leather top and a rosewood and sycamore box

2 Wooden hinged walnut box and rosewood treasure chest

3 *(Top)* Walnut box with sloping sides and ends and yew hexagonal box

4 *(Right)* Walnut writing box

9

TURNED BOXES

This chapter is not in any way a treatise on wood turning, there are plenty of those already on the bookshelves. However, this book would be incomplete without some mention of the possibilities of turning in the making of boxes. Colour plate 7 shows a selection of small turned boxes. They have one thing in common, they have all been made from scrap pieces of wood, the sort of bits which can so easily end up on the fire. Turning is a fascinating craft and one which brings results quickly, unlike the rest of the work described in this book which tends to be very labour-intensive. It is certainly refreshing to go to the lathe and spend a little while actually seeing the wood take shape in much the same way the potter sees the clay shape on his wheel.

Mounting the wood

The wood can be screwed directly to a face-plate, but this will leave screw holes in the bottom and will limit the depth to which it can be turned inside before the end of the screw is reached. Instead, it should be glued onto a piece of waste wood, which is itself screwed to the face plate. Do not glue it directly to the waste wood but glue a layer of tissue paper in the sandwich. The inclusion of the paper will make separation easy, since the tissue paper will split down its thickness when pressure is applied from a chisel. Just enter the chisel and tap with a mallet.

Turning

Mount the face plate on the lathe and bring up the tailstock centre to give extra support. Turn-up the outside, but do not go right down to the finished shape. Withdraw the tailstock centre and turn the inside to its finished shape. Now complete the outside turning, using sharp tools and light pressure. Glasspaper inside and out and polish but leave it still on its waste wood. Remove from the lathe.

Top

Mount the piece of wood for the top in the same way. In a small box let the lid overhang for easy gripping. Turn a rebate until it will just fit the opening to the box. It must be a really tight fit at this stage. Remove the top from its waste with a tap from a chisel.

Remount the box and push the lid well home. The rest of the lid can be turned in this position and finished off and polished.

Knob

If a knob is required, drill a hole on the lid using a drill held in the tail stock. ¼in. (6mm) drill will be adequate.

Remove the box from the lathe and turn the knob between centres, making a round tenon to match the hole size. Clean up and polish as much as possible and then saw it off and glue into the hole in the lid. Remount the box and complete the turning of the knob.

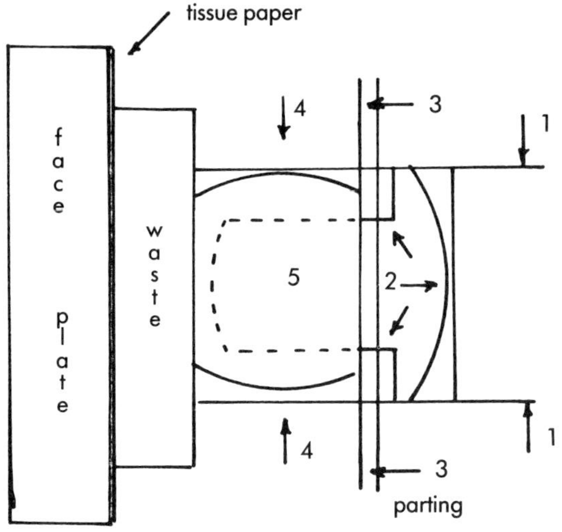

***Figure* 89** *Stages in turning the round box*

Finishing

Remove the box from its waste wood with a chisel and mallet. Complete the work by gluing a piece of baize or felt to the bottom.

Alternative method

The lid can be turned as a part of the box, providing there is enough wood. Mount the wood on the face-plate as above. Turn-up the outside until it is round. With a parting tool cut a collar where the lid will come (figure 89). Part off the lid. Turn the outside of the box and then the inside. Glasspaper inside and out. Keep fitting the lid which must be a tight fit. Push the lid tight home and complete its turning, clean up and polish the whole box. If a knob is required, proceed as in the first method. Complete with baize on the bottom.

two

WORKING WOOD

10

EQUIPMENT

BENCH

A good firm kitchen table and a portable vice will be adequate for most of the work in this book. A firm shelf across the end of a garage is better and naturally a specially designed bench is better still.

Figure 90 gives some ideas for a suitable bench. Good solid legs 4in. (120mm) square are essential. The top should be not less than 1½in. (38mm) and preferably 2in (50mm) thick. It need not be this thickness all the way across as the diagram shows. Using thinner wood has the added advantages of providing a well for the tools as well as reducing the cost. Wide apron pieces improve the stability of the bench enormously. Stretcher rails forming a shelf or cupboards built underneath will not only provide useful storage space but the extra weight will help to anchor the bench.

The vice is fitted so that the metal top is about ½in (12mm) below the surface of the bench. This will mean cutting out a piece from the top to let the inner metal jaw come flush with the edge of the bench top. Secure the vice with coach screws to the underside of the top. If the top is not thick enough it will be necessary to use a piece of wood as packing to take up the spare.

Wooden vice-jaws are added, see figure 90. They are fastened to the vice with bolts with their heads countersunk below the surface of the jaws. It is these jaws which do the actual holding and for this reason they must be well maintained. If they are rough, they will mark the surface of the wood they are holding, if worn

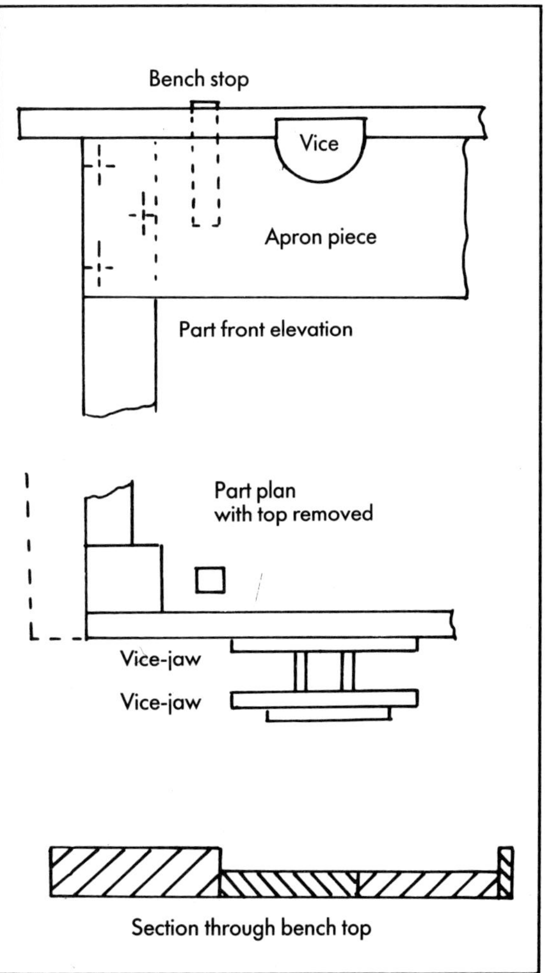

Figure 90 *Details of bench*

Figure 91 *A group of handmade tools. From back to front; simple scratch stock, veneering hammer, two dovetail templates and another scratch stock*

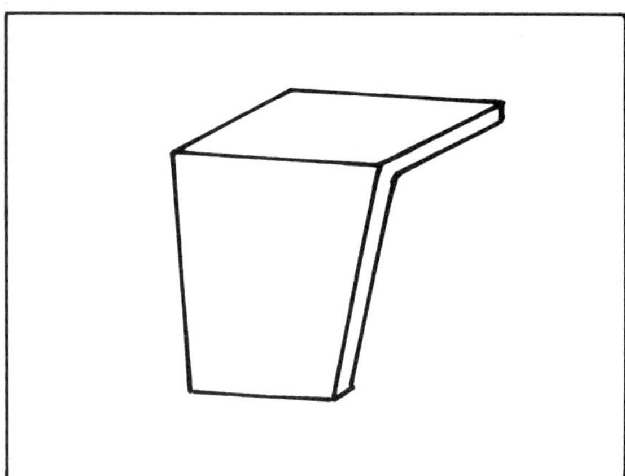

Figure 92 *Dovetail templates*

they will not grip effectively.

The bench stop must be made to fit tightly into the bench top. It can then be raised and lowered with the tap of a hammer. It should be about 1½in (38mm) square. Expensive ones can be bought which run alonside the leg of the bench and are held in place with a wing nut but these are not essential. As an alternative, a strip of wood can be screwed across the bench with the screws deeply countersunk. This tends to get in the way and the thickness cannot be changed without screwing on another strip.

SELECTION OF TOOLS

This is very difficult, but the aim is to suggest a minimum of tools required to make the boxes and chests and so keep costs down.

Essential tools

6in. try square
Marking knife
12in. steel ruler
Marking gauge
Cutting gauge
10in. tenon saw
Sliding bevel
4½in. mallet
8oz Warrington hammer
Screwdriver
Bradawl
Coping saw
Oil stone (two sided)
Pincers
Jack plane
Combination or shoulder plane
Plough plane (small one adequate)
Flat spokeshave
Cork block
Hand drill
¼in. bevel-edge chisel
½in. firmer chisel
⅛in. firmer chisel
Vice
4 × 24in. sash cramps
2 × 6in. 'G' cramps

Additional helpful tools

Round spokeshave
Rebate plane or side fillister
Rip saw
Mitre square
Cross cut saw
Emery wheel and/or grindstone

Machine Router (portable)

Items to be made

Bench
Bench hook
Dovetail template
Veneering hammer
Scratch stock
45 degree jig
Chiselling board

TOOLS TO BE MADE

Bench hook or sawing board

Two pieces of wood 1½in (38mm) square are screwed across a piece of 1in (25mm) thick wood. The holes for the screws are counter-bored so that the screw heads will be well below the surface. The holes can then be filled with wood. The bench hook protects the bench from saw cuts. It provides a way of holding the wood securely while it is being sawn, and supports the wood so that when the saw goes through, pieces do not break off (see figure 120). Beech is a good wood to use.

Dovetail template

A dovetail slopes at an angle of 1:7. This can be set on a sliding bevel but it is more convenient to make a metal template. Figure 91 shows two

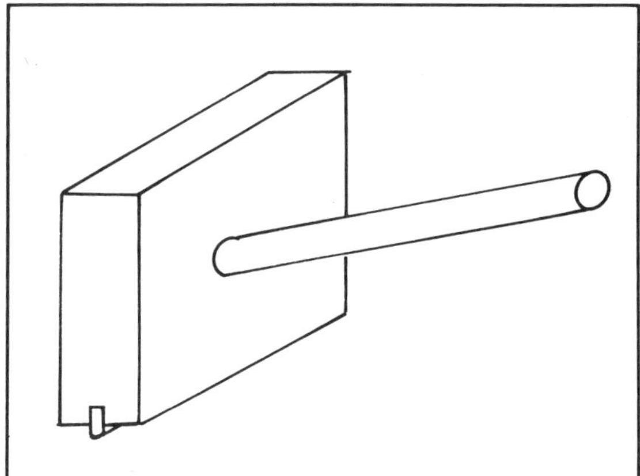

Figure 93 *Veneering hammer*

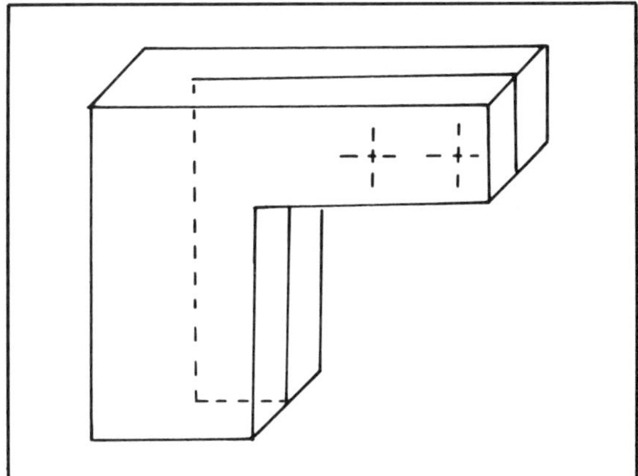

Figure 94 *Scratch stock*

different shapes. The details of the left-hand one are shown in figure 92. Any odd scrap of metal-sheet can be used for this purpose.

Veneering hammer

This consists of a piece of wood with a brass insert and a handle made of dowel-rod, set in at an angle for ease of operation. The exposed edge of the brass should be carefully rounded-off, otherwise it will damage the veneer (figures 91 and 93).

Scratch stock

At the back left of figure 91 there is a very crude but effective scratch stock, whilst in the front is a more sophisticated one. The first will do the work admirably. Take an 'L' shaped piece of wood 1in (25mm) thick and saw down the middle through the narrow section and well into the butt. Drill clearance holes through one half, so that screws will have the effect of tightening together the narrow strips and holding the scratch stock blade in place (see figure 94). The blades are made from old machine hacksaw blades, (one old blade will last a lifetime). The blades are ground or filed to shape and left square across their ends. The photograph gives sufficient detail for anyone to make the other scratch stock.

45 degree jig

Beech is the most suitable timber, preferably 1in. (25mm) thick. Plane one end to an angle of 45 degrees and screw a strip of wood along the edge at right-angles to this edge. The wood to be mitred can be held tightly against this strip. The whole set up is held in the vice (figure 95).

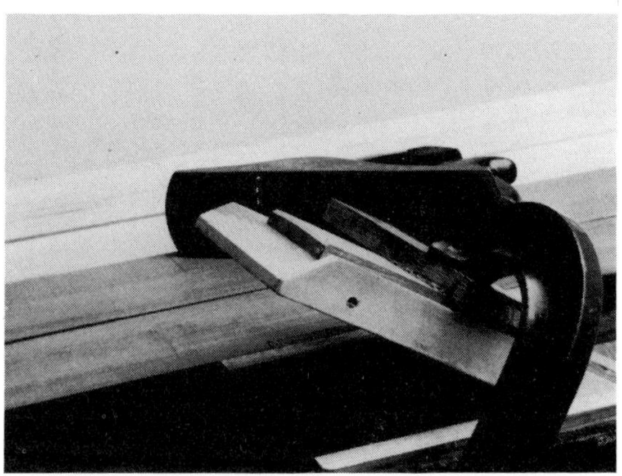

Figure 95 *Jig for planing mitres. The box end being mitred is held in position on the jig with a 'G' cramp*

Chiselling board

A flat board is required to rest the wood on when vertically paring. If the wood is not held firmly down on a flat surface it will not be cut cleanly. It is a good idea to keep a piece of wood specially for this purpose, occasionally re-planing the surface. Beech would be excellent for this.

Figure 96 *Portable machine router*

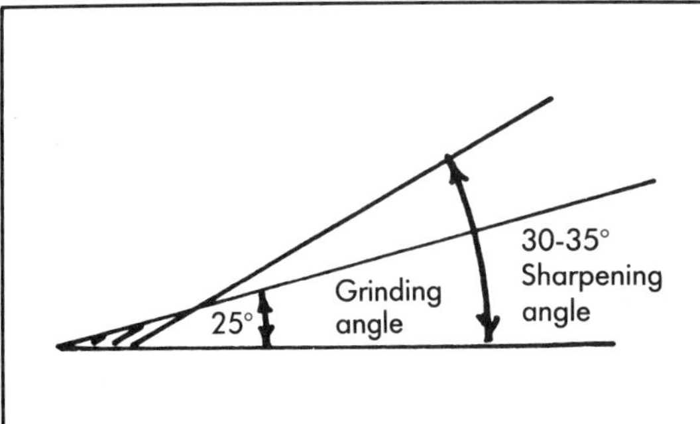

Figure 97 *Grinding and sharpening angles*

MACHINE ROUTER

A portable machine router is an expensive but very versatile tool (figure 96). It can be used in a variety of ways. At its simplest it can be used like a plough plane. Working from the edge of the wood it can rebate, groove and mould by merely changing the cutter.

It can be used across the grain and is the best way of making housings. Take a piece of waste wood and cramp a batten across it. Fit the correct sized bit. *Always unplug before changing bits.* Run across the waste. This will give the distance between the edge of the bit and the batten. It will also show the depth which has been set. Take the wood to be housed and 'G' cramp a batten at exactly the same distance away as the trial piece. The router will make a stopped housing as easily as a through one.

To make a curve it is necessary to make a template. Screw the bush follower plate on the router and make the template so that this will slide easily in it. This sort of template is illustrated in figure 68 where it is used to make a tambour box.

SHARPENING

This is essential if tools are to work satisfactorily. Blunt chisels are not only ineffective, they are positively dangerous.

Plane iron

Sharpening a plane iron

Remove the blade from the plane and unscrew the cap iron. The blade has two angles, a grinding and a sharpening angle (figure 97). A freshly ground plane requires only a few rubs to restore its sharpness, but after a while the amount of metal to be worn off gets too much and the blade has to be re-ground. Figure 97 shows how this area increases with successive sharpenings.

Grinding causes a lot of trouble because of the lack of additional expensive equipment. What is ideally required is a water-cooled, motorised wheel. This will have a guide which can be set to the correct grinding angle of 25 degrees and the blade can be ground without any danger of drawing the temper and softening the blade. The next best thing is a carborundum wheel but this has the disadvantage that unless it is a big machine the wheel is not very thick. This makes it difficult to grind a really flat surface and generates a lot of heat. It is very easy to loose the temper and finish up with a soft edge to the blade. If both machines are ruled out, buy a double-sided carborundum stone, one side rough and the other smooth and use the rough side for the grinding angle. It is, however, not a good solution.

The sharpening angles do not present any difficulty. Rest the blade on the oilstone at the

Figure 98 *Sharpening a plane blade*

Figure 99 *Removing the burr from the back of the plane blade*

Figure 100 *Using a plough plane with the wood secured to the bench with a 'G' cramp*

Figure 101 *Using a plough plane with the wood held in a sash cramp which is itself held, with wooden blocks on each side, in the vice*

grinding angle and raise it a further 10 degrees. Keep this constant angle and run backwards and forwards until a burr can be felt on the edge of the blade (figure 98). Turn the blade over and, holding it flat on the stone, rub it up and down the stone to remove the burr (figure 99). Repeat the operation until the edge is sharp. Use the full length of the stone so that it will stay flat.

Chisels

Chisels are sharpened in the same way. This time, try and use the full width as well as the full length of the oil stone.

Spokeshave

The same technique is required. Because they are rather short spokeshave blades are a little harder to hold than most blades.

PLOUGH PLANE

A plough plane has two settings apart from the blade. The distance it operates in from the edge of a board is controlled by a fence (figure 100). This can be adjusted by slackening two thumbscrews. A depth-stop is fitted on the opposite side of the plane. As the plane settles in the groove it is making, the depth stop gets nearer the surface of the wood until it runs along the surface. When this happens the plane can go no deeper. It can be set to the required depth before planing commences. In figure 101 it has not yet quite touched the wood.

The wood, if it is wide enough, can be held in place on the bench with a 'G' cramp (figure 100). If it is too narrow for this, then hold it between the jaws of a sash cramp, which is itself held in a vice. Notice the two packing pieces on either side of the cramp (figure 101).

Select the correct blade and set it to remove a fine shaving. Set the fence and the depth-stop and start planing at the far end of the wood. With a shuffling action gradually work a way down the length of the wood. As the groove grows deeper the depth-stop will rub along the surface and stop the plane from working when the right depth has been reached.

SHOULDER AND COMBINATION PLANE

A shoulder plane is shown in figure 78. It is capable of very delicate work. The fingers take the part of the fence in the plough plane. The blade is set at a very low angle so it has less tendency to split the end grain provided it is sharp and set fine. Working on boxes it can be used where a side fillister would operate on larger jobs.

The combination plane is a more elaborate form of the shoulder plane. Two fronts are supplied which can be screwed in place. Without either the plane is a chisel plane, with the smaller front a bull-nosed plane, and with the larger a shoulder plane. These different arrangements make it possible to get into difficult positions more easily.

CHISELS

These can be purchased as the occasion demands. Always buy the best on the market. An 1/8in. (3mm) bevel-edged chisel will be useful for small dovetails and a larger, firmer chisel would also be an advantage.

11

TIMBER

Like all living things a tree consists of cells, of which the majority are arranged so that they run up and down the length of the tree. The tree starts as a single stem which increases in length and girth each year. It grows by cell division in a layer which occurs just beneath the bark. At the same time as new cells are produced old cells die. The band of living cells under the bark are termed the sapwood and the dead cells which form the bulk of a fully grown tree are the heartwood. The band of sapwood will remain the same width as the tree grows but the proportion of heartwood will steadily increase as cells continue to die. At intervals branches will spring from the growing tip forming knots in the trunk.

THE STRUCTURE OF WOOD

Bark

Some of the cells will divide and become bark, forming a protective coat round the tree. These too will die so there is also live and dead bark. The dead layer sometimes flakes off, or it remains on the tree and has to expand by cracking as the tree increases in girth.

Sapwood

The sapwood contains starch and is usually lighter in colour and weight than the heartwood. It is usually softer as well. In walnut the sapwood is white, while the heartwood is all shades of brown. The sapwood should be discarded since the starch makes it particularly attractive to woodworm. Figure 75 shows the sapwood in laburnum.

Seasoning

This is touched on in Chapter 7 dealing with oyster veneering. The subject is too big to be dealt with in detail. A tree contains its own weight of sap when it is growing. This will start drying out as soon as the tree is felled and will continue until it matches up with the atmosphere. At first only moisture from inside the cell dries out and no change in size takes place. During the second stage moisture dries out from the cell walls. Since these are long and thin the change affects the cross section, but has little or no effect on the length. No attempt must be made to use the wood until it has dried out to match the moisture content of its destination. This means that for centrally heated rooms the timber must be drier than for a cooler situation.

As the local situation changes from summer to winter, from very dry to very wet, the wood will continue to take in or give out moisture and so expand or contract. It is this movement which creates most of the problems which come from the use of wood.

Wood also has a natural tendency to warp or curve. The exterior of the tree contains the most moisture and so will shrink the most during seasoning. This applies to individual boards, the side nearest the outside of the tree will shrink more than the inside face and the wood will try to bow away from the heart (figure 102). During seasoning a stack of timber is weighted down to prevent this movement. Wood must be used in such a way that it can expand and contract but not warp. A good example of how this can be done is seen in a panelled construction (figure 103). Here the panel is held in a frame to prevent it warping and a gap is left between the panel and the bottom of the groove to allow for any expansion.

Short grain

The fact that the cells run up and down the tree and are long and thin means that wood is strong about its length and weak about its width. A floor joist needs to have the grain parallel to its length and even a slight deviation will make it weak and liable to fail when under stress (figure 104). Any short grain will make for weak joints and difficulty in working that piece of wood. This fact dictates that the wood for a box must be arranged so that the grain runs round the box (figure 105). It also means that dovetails must be made on the end of a piece of wood and not the side (figure 106).

Figured boards

These are boards which have a particularly attractive grain. Figure comes about in different ways depending on whether the wood is a softwood or a hardwood (figure 107).

(i) Figured softwood

In softwoods, which have a simpler structure than hardwoods, the cells get squashed up towards the end of the growing season in autumn. This produces the pronounced growth rings which are seen in a cross section. It is these growth rings which produce the 'figure' or pattern in soft wood. If the board is sawn to show off these rings along the face of the board then it will be figured. Figures 108 and 109 show plain and figured softwood respectively.

(ii) Figured hardwood

Things are not quite so clear-cut in hardwoods but, in the main, growth rings are minor features. Their cellular structure is more complex than that of softwoods and they have cells which radiate out from the growing area just under the bark, towards the centre of the tree in the form of plates. They have depth down the tree as well as length from the outside inwards. Some of these bands of cells will reach right to the

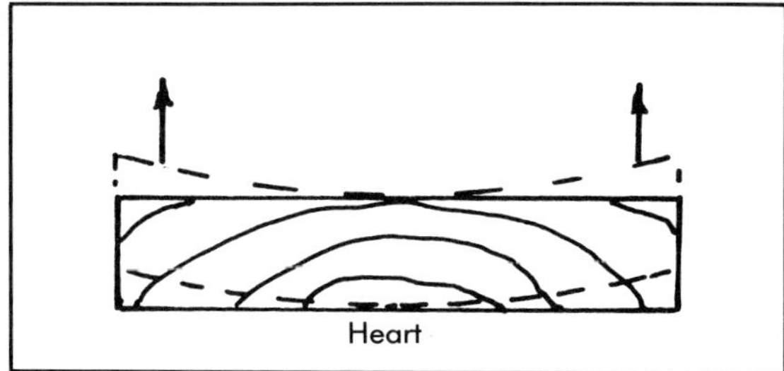

Figure 102 *Warp*

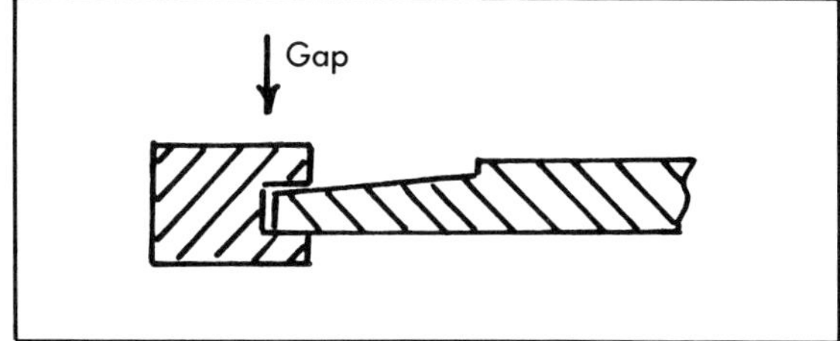

Figure 103 *Panelled construction*

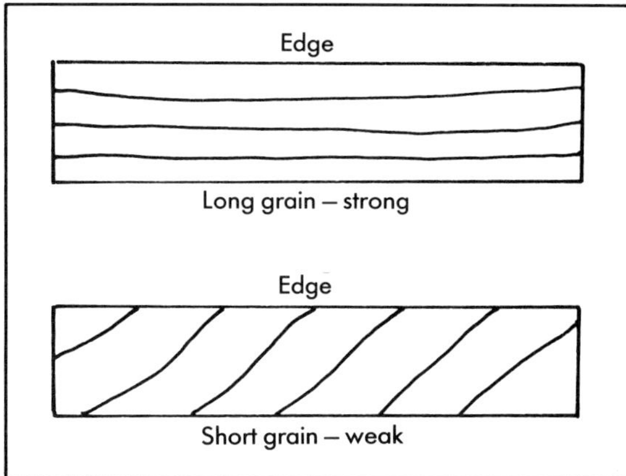

Figure 104 *Long and short grain*

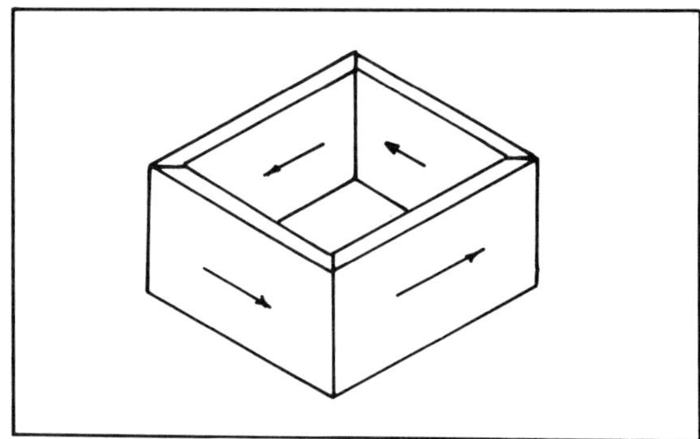

Figure 105 *Grain must run round box*

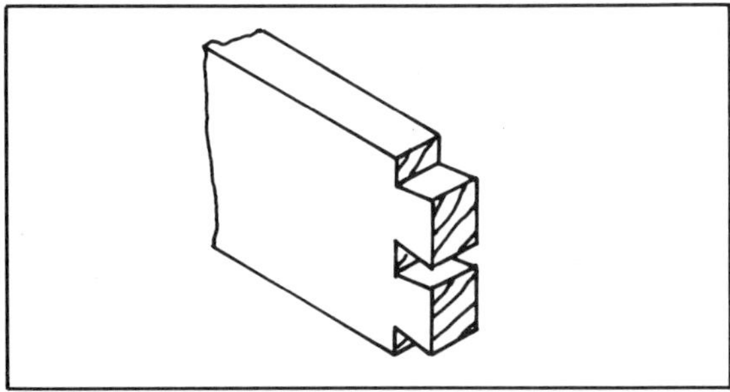

Figure **106** *Dovetail on the end*

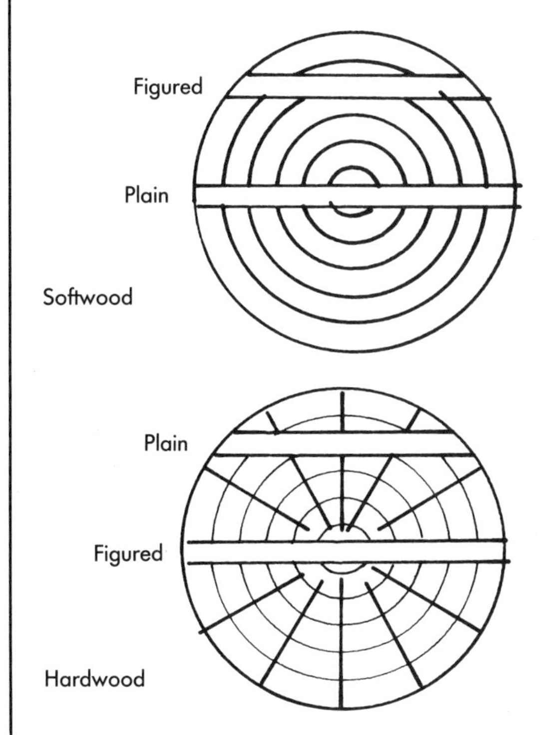

Figure **107** *Figured boards*

Figure **108** *Plain deal*

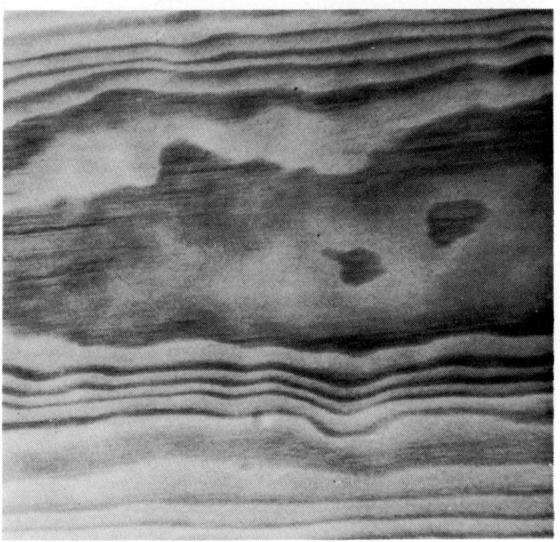

Figure **109** *Figured deal*

centre, some will stop short. These cells are called medullary rays and they provide the figure in hardwoods. (Softwoods also have medullary rays but these are usually invisible to the naked eye.) These rays are especially large in oak where the resulting pattern is sometimes called flower. Figures 110 and 111 show plain and figured oak respectively.

Burrs

Some trees get a disease and produce a growth on the side of the trunk. These lumps are called burrs and can reach a diameter of six feet. Inside, the burr consists of a mass of tiny knots. Some burrs are very coarse and contain as much air as wood, others are much finer and are in great demand for veneers. Figure 112 shows

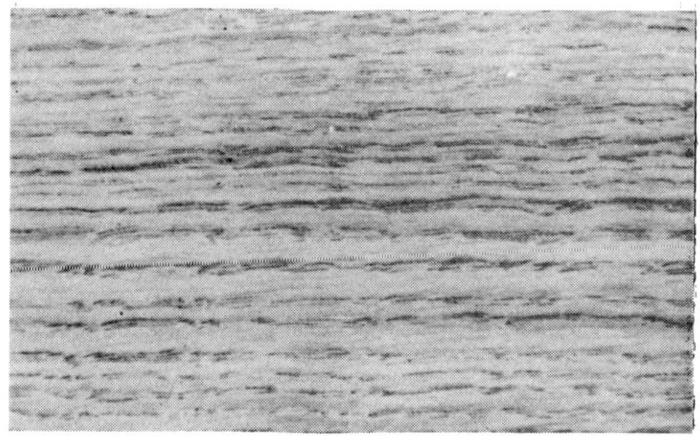

***Figure* 110** *Plain oak*

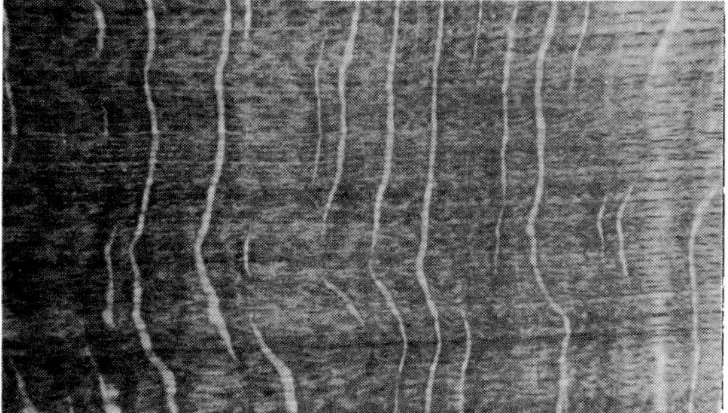

***Figure* 111** *Figured oak*

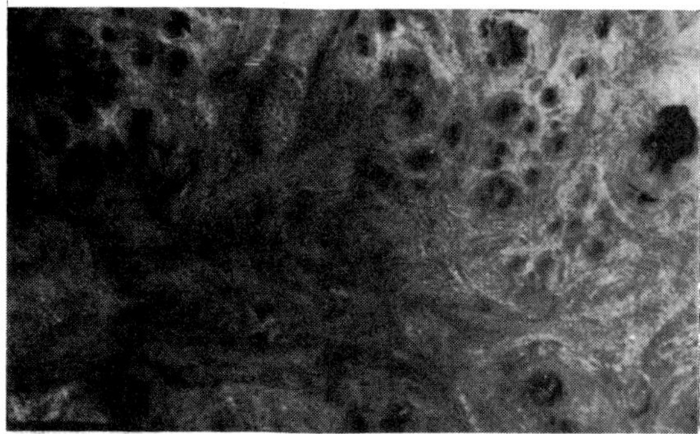

***Figure* 112** *Burr elm*

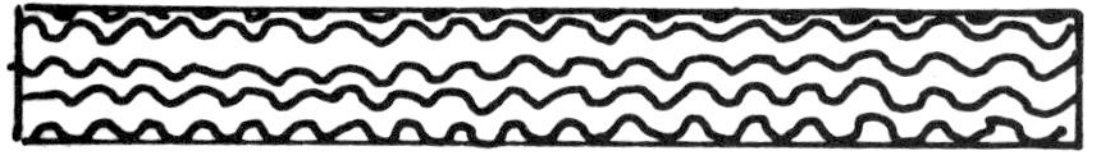

***Figure* 113** *Wavy grain producing ripple*

a piece of burr elm. Colour plate 5 shows a box covered with burr walnut veneer.

Grain

Wood is fascinating because no two pieces are ever alike in colour or grain. The craftsmans job is to use wood to its best advantage, for nature has provided a beautiful material.

There are one or two special features which are worth looking out for. Particularly attractive grain may come about for several reasons. It could be an abnormality like burrs. It could be the position in the tree, butt grain or crutch grain. It could be the way the wood was sawn up, as with figured wood. It could be the characteristic of a particular tree's growth, as with stripy grain. It is worth noting that the more difficult the grain and the harder it is to produce a polished surface, the more attractive is the likely result. Hard work will certainly bring its reward.

Butt grain

The wood from the area nearest the ground, the butt of the log, seems to change in texture and grain markings, especially in walnut. This makes a very attractive wood with an eccentric grain resulting in some loss of strength. Not a wood to make dovetails in. It can, however still be used, see colour plate 6. All the drawer fronts came out of the same piece of wood and so the grain markings continue right down the front of the chest. Because it is unsuitable for jointing, it was glued onto another piece of wood with normal grain and the joints were made in that.

Stripy grain

A number of tropical hardwoods have an interlocking grain. This is caused by cells running in a spiral round the trunk and reversing direction every few years producing stripes on the face of the wood. Since this means a change in direction of the grain, it makes planing and cleaning-up difficult. The top in figure 42 is made from utile a West African timber which has these stripes.

Crutch grain

When a stem divides into two an especially beautiful grain is formed, giving an unusual effect. It is most dramatic if it is sawn as a cross section and figure 75 shows this grain exploited

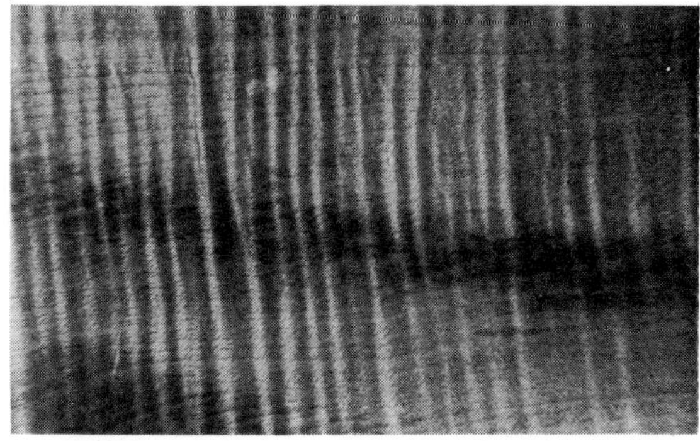

Figure 114 *Sycamore with a ripple grain*

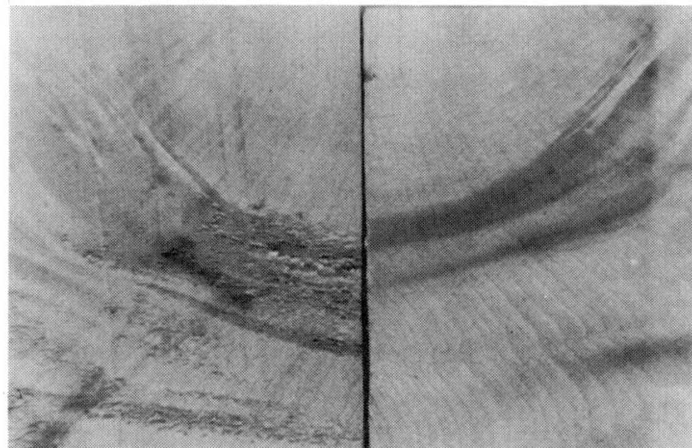

Figure 115 *Before and after. Sycamore showing the confused state of the grain before and after planing*

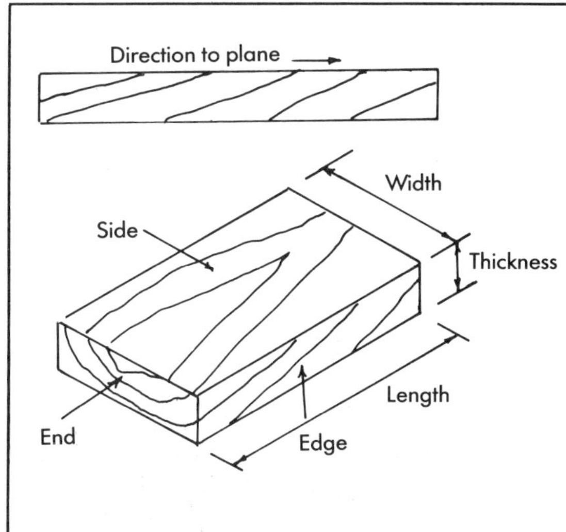

Figure 116 *Terminology and grain direction*

as a laburnum oyster. It could, and this is more general, be split longitudinally with very interesting results.

Ripple grain

Ripple is caused by a wavy grain, (see figure 113). The result is a very attractive piece of wood (figure 114). Figure 115 is a before and after photograph. This example of ripple is sycamore. On the left is the result of some coarse machine planing which highlights the confused state of the grain. On the right is the wood after it has been cleaned up with a very sharp plane.

TIMBER PREPARATION

Terminology

Length is always measured along the grain, from end to end. The width and thickness are always measured across the grain with the width being the larger of the two (figure 116). If the measurements are the same then it does not matter which is which.

A piece of wood has two sides which contain the width, and two edges containing the thickness. The two ends represent a cross section of the tree and show the growth rings.

Planing

Assuming the wood to be 'rough' that is, left from the saw all the way round there is a recognised method of attack. First plane one side, then an edge then the second edge followed by the second side. The ends require special treatment. Here is the process in more detail using a box as an example.

Take a piece of wood which is long enough to make two sides and two ends. It should be 1/4in. (6mm) wider, 1/8in. (3.2mm) thicker and 15/16in. (24mm) longer than the finished width and thickness and the combined lengths respectively. The extra material will allow for waste resulting from planing and sawing.

1 Choose the best of the two sides. With this uppermost, place it flat on the bench against the bench stop, having looked at the edge to find out the right direction to plane (figure 116). Plane with the jack plane until the side is smooth and flat. Test the flatness with the edge of a steel ruler across the width about

the length and from corner to corner. The latter is to make sure that the wood is not twisted or 'in wind' (see page 66 for explanation). When satisfied place the face mark on the side with its tail pointing towards the best edge.

2 Hold the wood in the vice with the best edge uppermost and plane it. This time test that it is flat about its length with the edge of the steel ruler and at right angles to the face side with a try square. When the edge is accurate mark it with a 'V' pointing to the face side.

3 Use the marking gauge to gauge the width, pressing the gauge tightly against the face edge (figure 117). Mark both sides. With the wood in the vice, plane down to the gauge line.

4 Gauge to thickness and with the wood in the vice, plane down to the gauge line.

The whole sequence of operations is shown in figure 118.

***Figure* 117** *Using a marking gauge*

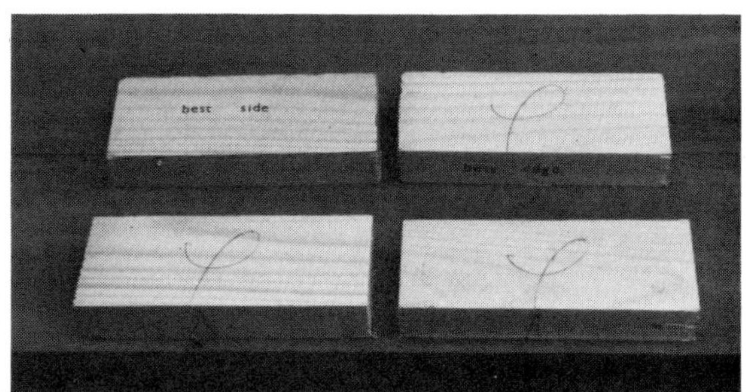

***Figure* 118** *Planing*

T L choose best side. Plane it
TR Choose best edge. Plane it
BL Gauge to width and plane
BR Gauge to thickness and plane

Marking out and sawing to length

To mark out the four separate pieces, put the wood in the vice with the face edge uppermost. Using a try square, marking knife and steel ruler measure in 3⁄16in. (5mm) from one end, then the finished length of a side, then 3⁄16in. (5mm) followed by the second side, a similar gap and the first end, a gap and, finally, the second end. There will be a similar piece of waste at this end of the wood. The waste at intervals is to allow for the saw cuts and squaring the ends. Take the wood out of the vice and square the lines all the way round using the try square and marking knife (figure 119). The use of the knife instead of a pencil will give cleaner and more accurate results.

Place the wood on a sawing board held in the vice (figure 120). Hold the wood against it and saw carefully. The knife line should be just visible on the sawn end. (For details of how to make a sawing board see Chapter 10.)

***Figure* 119** *Squaring around the end using a try square against the face edge*

Ends

Because of a wood's cellular nature, ends require special treatment. If a plane is allowed to go right across the ends it will cause them to split. Figure 121 shows a simple arrangement which will prevent this happening. A piece of wood (or planing stop) is put behind the piece to be planed. This planing stop should be the same

Figure **120** *Lengths squared round with a marking knife*

Figure **121** *Planing end grain using a planing stop*

Figure **122** *Testing the end using a try square against the face edge*

Figure **123** *Testing the end using a try square against the face side*

thickness or thicker than the piece to be planed, and should have its top corner sawn off to stop it from splitting. This is set up across the vice so that the vice holds them tightly together. Work to the cut line. Take the wood out of the vice and test the end with a try square in two directions, (see figures 122 and 123).

If the wood is too wide to fit in the vice this way, then it is wide enough to adopt another method. Hold the wood in the vice and plane in from each edge working about two thirds of the way each time but never right across. Test in two directions.

Machine planed

Imported hardwoods tend to be planed on two sides. However, a machine planer leaves parallel lines across the wood and is not very accurate within the scale of small boxes. Treat the wood as unplaned but very little will have to be removed from the two sides.

Planing mitres

To mitre the ends use the jig seen in figure 95 and described in Chapter 10. Notice how the wood is held tightly against the jig and the whole thing held in the vice. It must be remembered that the jig is only a guide which will become inaccurate with use and will itself require checking each time it is used. Plane down to the line and remove the wood. Test with a sliding bevel set to 45 degrees or a mitre square.

Edge joining

It frequently happens that the available wood is not wide enough. This is overcome by gluing the two pieces edge to edge. If the grain and colour are similar the glue line will be hardly visible. Mark the direction to plane with an arrow on each piece of wood and arrange them to give the best match but having the arrows in the same direction. In this way when the pieces are

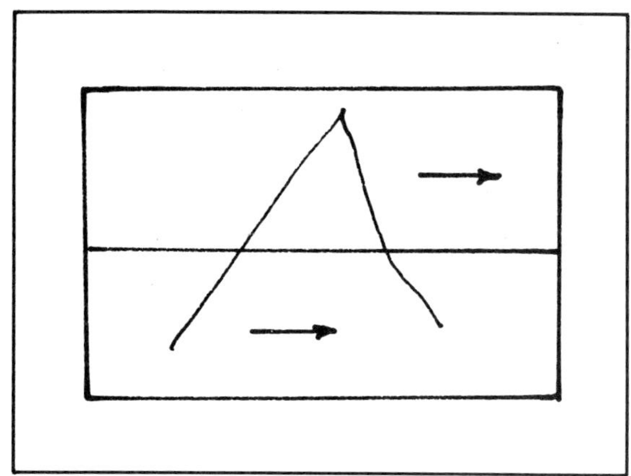

Figure 124 *Edge joining*

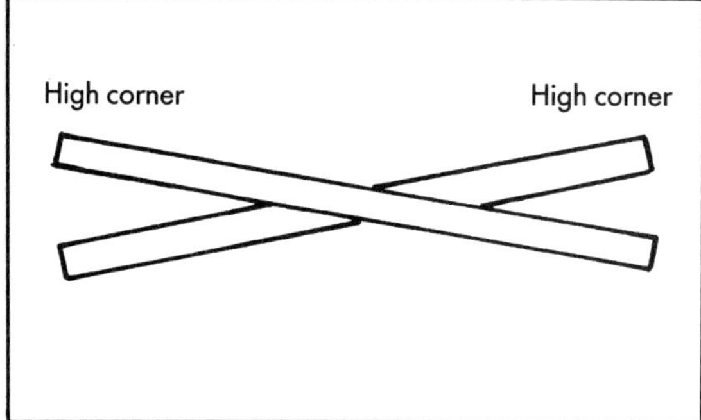

Figure 125 *An exaggerated view of wind*

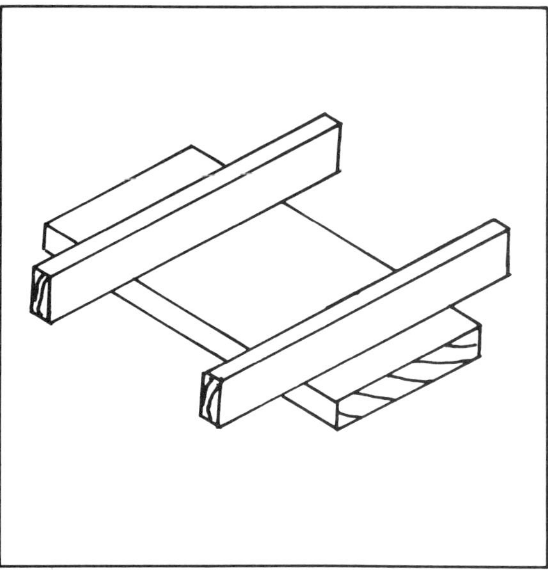

Figure 126 *Winding strips in place*

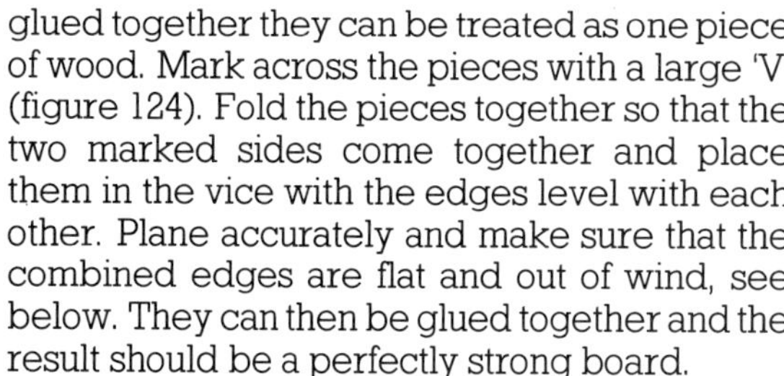

glued together they can be treated as one piece of wood. Mark across the pieces with a large 'V' (figure 124). Fold the pieces together so that the two marked sides come together and place them in the vice with the edges level with each other. Plane accurately and make sure that the combined edges are flat and out of wind, see below. They can then be glued together and the result should be a perfectly strong board.

Wind

This is the name given to a twist in a piece of wood. This is not a big problem while the sizes of material are small but will arise more frequently with larger boxes. The amount of wind across the face of a board can be tested by using a ruler across the corners. A more accurate way is to use winding strips. These are simply two strips of wood which have been planed parallel. Rest them across the wood and look down them. If they are in line with each other all is well, if not then the wood is in wind. This is corrected by planing from high corner to high corner (figure 125). Similarly, when long edge joints are made, these too should be tested. Figure 126 shows a side being tested.

Winding strips are simply parallel strips of wood. It is usual to choose two stable pieces of wood and keep them specially for this job. Their length exaggerates the error and makes it very easy to see.

12

CONSTRUCTIONS

PANEL PINS AND NAILS

Figure 127 shows a panel pin, an oval nail and a round nail. All are sold by length and gauge (thickness). The general rule for maximum strength is to use nails which are two and a half times the thickness of the top piece of wood. Nails are least effective when driven into end grain.

Panel pins

The shape of the head means that they can be easily punched below the surface. When joining two pieces of wood together with panel pins it helps if all the pins are driven into the top piece of wood until they just come through the wood. If glue is applied to the second piece the points will help to locate the top piece while the pins are being driven in.

Panel pins make useful small drills when their heads are cut off. They are especially useful for making pilot holes for small screws.

Nails

These are limited to quite crude work. The round heads have more holding power but the oval heads will go below the surface. When using oval nails knock them in with the maximum width across the grain of the wood. This will make them less likely to split the wood.

Splitting is one of the problems with nails. Two things can be done to help prevent this. Blunt the end of the nail by hammering it. This way it will tend to punch a hole in the wood rather than acting like a wedge. The other solution is to grease the nail before using it.

If the nails have to be driven into end grain use them like dovetails, see Chapter 1.

SCREWS

The two shapes of head used in this book are shown in figure 127, countersunk and round head. Each of these come in a variety of lengths and gauges. Except for the rougher boxes these will normally be brass.

All screws require two holes. The first, clearance hole, through the top piece of wood, should be large enough for the screw to be loose in it. The second piece of wood requires a thread hole. This is half the diameter of the first one. The second hole is often made with a bradawl. The following table gives the correct

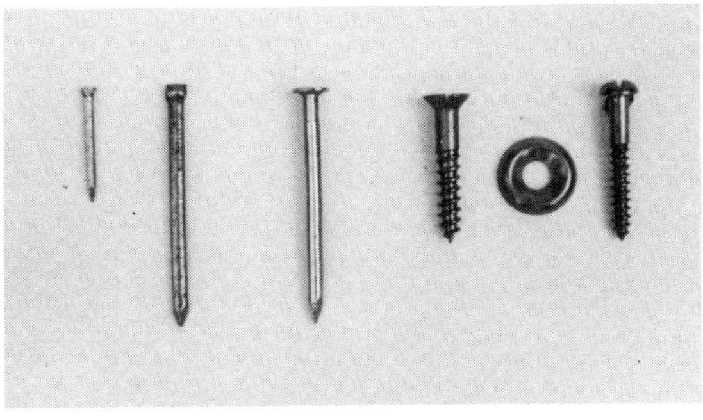

Figure 127 *From left to right: Panel pin, oval nail, round head nail, countersunk head screw, brass screw cup, brass round-head screw*

sizes for some of the gauges of screws.

Screw gauge (in.)	4	6	8
Clearance	1/8	5/32	3/16
Thread	1/16	5/64	3/32

Screw gauge (mm)	4	6	8
Clearance	3.2	4	4.8
Thread	1.6	2	2.4

If countersunk screws are used then the clearance holes must be countersunk using a drill and countersink bit to enable the screw to finish flush with the wood. Brass screws and brass screw-cups will improve the general appearance of the work, (figures 1 and 127).

As with nails the general rule of thumb is to choose screws two and a half times as long as the thickness of the top piece of wood.

All screws go in easier if a little wax is put on the thread. Oak is especially hard, therefore use a steel screw first and then replace with a brass one.

The gauge of the screw should match the thickness of the wood being used. Boxes with sides 3/8in. (10mm) thick require gauges 4 or 6.

REBATES

A rebate, is removed to allow for a bottom panel or, on the edge of a lid, to hold it in position. It is difficult to work because it is sometimes with the grain and sometimes against it and the method used has to take this into account (figure 128).

Rebates can always be sawn which ever way the grain. The rebate can then be planed with a shoulder plane until the line is reached.

Rebates with the grain, plane easily with a shoulder plane. This plane can also be used across the grain with care it it is set fine .

A side fillister plane is designed to work either rebate. Ahead of the blade is a side cutter held in with a screw. It has three small blades in the form of a trefoil. Slacken the screw and allow one blade to stick below the surface of the plane. When the plane is used across the grain this cutter will sever the fibres of the wood ahead of the blade and prevent them tearing. Replace the side cutter when using the plane with the grain.

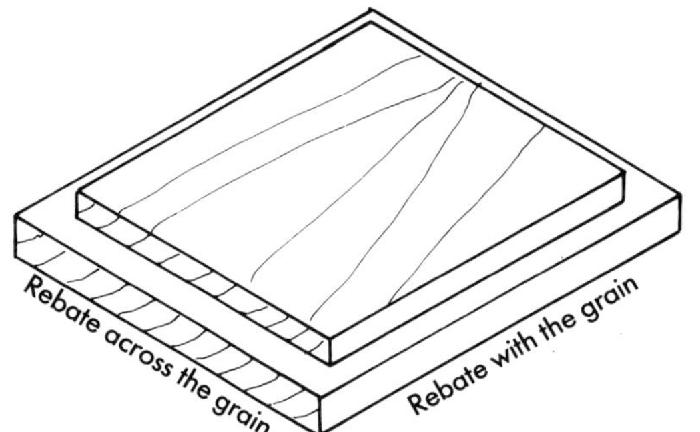

***Figure* 128** *Rebated bottom*

GROOVES

These are always with the grain and require a plough plane (figure 129). If the grain runs across the groove so that the plough leaves a very rough groove it will help if a cutting gauge is set so that it cuts two lines down each side of the groove before the plough is used.

HOUSING

This is always across the grain. Using hand methods the sides of the housing must be sawn first. The waste can be removed with a chisel or, if available, a hand router. (These appear to have been taken off the market or they would be on the tool list.) A chisel will work perfectly so long as the housing is not too wide.

The housing is an example of where a machine can do a better job. Controlled by a batten or fence secured across the wood, it takes the waste out cleanly in any direction. It is also easily stopped at either end.

CLAMPING

A clamp across a narrow piece of wood consists of a groove down the batten, made with a plough plane, and a double rebate across the grain on each edge of the centre board. The rebate can be worked with a side fillister plane, or by sawing followed by a shoulder plane, or just using a shoulder plane.

The wider clamp involves mortise and tenon (figure 17). This is a joint which does not really come within the scope of this book. It is not difficult but ideally it would require a mortise gauge, which has two points, one of which is adjustable, and a mortise chisel, a particularly strong chisel designed to withstand continuous malleting.

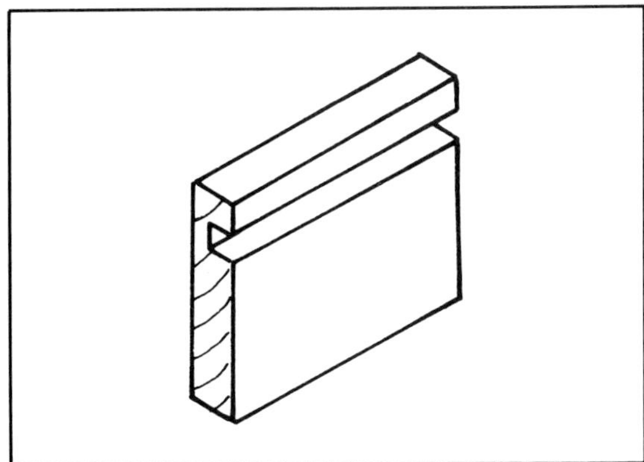

Figure 129 *Groove for sliding lid*

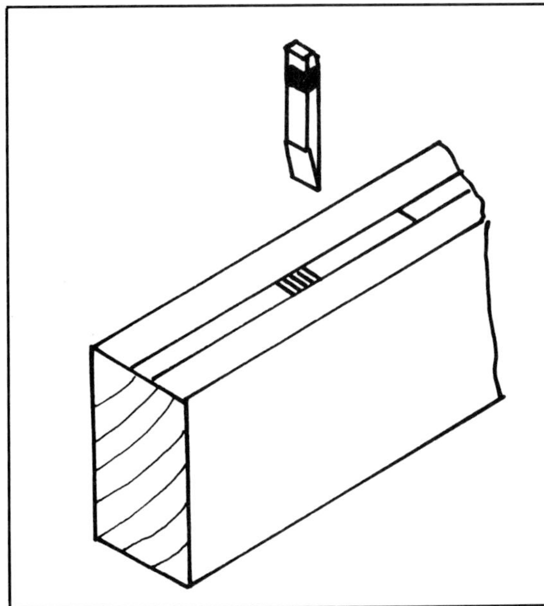

Figure 130 *Removal of mortise hole by chopping*

Using the listed tools, mark out using a marking gauge. If this is set carefully the same setting can be used working from both sides of the wood. A firmer chisel can be used to chop out the mortises if reasonable care is taken (figure 130). Put a strip of plaster round the end of the chisel to mark the depth. Then chisel out the slope at each end and chop out the housing in the middle. The tenons are made with a saw. Saw down the grain first. Remove the centre portion with a coping saw.

DOVETAILS

Making a good through dovetail is very satisfying, but it is also very taxing and one of the most difficult joints to make. However, it becomes easier with practise and dovetails really do look very attractive.

Through dovetails

The following method shows how well-fitting dovetail joints can be made every time. It assumes that the sides and ends of a small box have been planed and the ends squared so that they are ready to receive the dovetails.

Arrange the sides and ends in the shape of a box and letter each corner, **A**, **B**, **C** and **D** so that each half of each joint has the same letter. Set the cutting gauge to the thickness of the wood and gauge round each end of each piece.

Find the side with **A** on it and put it in the vice with end **A** uppermost. This is represented by figure 131a. Mark out the arrangement of tails and pins. For a start make the pins ¼in. (6mm) and keep the tails under 1in. (25mm). Experience will soon show which look right. Imagine a side 2⅜in. (60mm) wide, three pins ¼in. (6mm) each will leave two tails ⅞in. (21mm). If in doubt draw the proposed arrangement full sized on paper and this will show exactly what the finished arrangement will look like, figure 131b.

Use a template to draw the dovetail shape down each side and mark the pieces which are to be removed.

Saw down the lines on the waste side of the line, (figure 131d). Remove most of the centre waste with a coping saw and finish by paring on a chiselling board with a bevel-edged chisel. (A firmer chisel will damage the sides of the tails.) With the wood in the vice remove the corners leaving a little to be pared off using a chisel. The tails are now complete (figure 131e).

The next stage involves marking out using the tails which have just been made. Take the end **A** and put it in the vice protruding the thickness of a piece of waste wood (figure 132). Slide the waste wood away and rest side **A** on to the end in the vice and the waste wood. This arrangement makes a bridge and makes it easier to hold the wood which will be less likely to move during the marking out. Line up the two ends marked **A** exactly and press firmly down. Using a sharp knife draw round the tails. A knife is

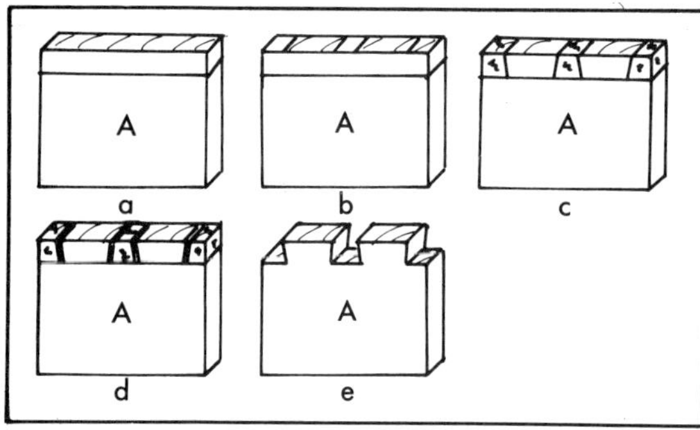

Figure 131 *Method for making well-fitting dovetail joints*

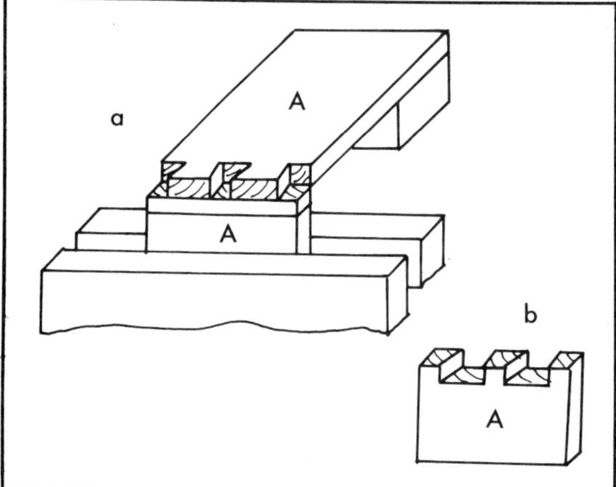

Figure 132 *(a) Marking out the pins. (b) Completed pins*

essential to get an accurate shape. Take the end out of the vice and square the markings down the sides with a try square. Repeat the operation with the other three corners. Mark the waste.

Place one of the ends in the vice and saw down to the cutting gauge line. Remove the bulk of the waste with a coping saw and finally pare down on the chiselling board, (figure 132). Finally fit each joint.

The joints are lettered on the outside to ensure that none of the sides or ends get turned round. Interior marks will be erased during cleaning up before gluing so without exterior lettering there will be no way of knowing which joint fits where.

Mitres

Mitres can be worked on either the top, bottom or both edges. Go around the ends with a cutting gauge as before, then set a marking gauge to

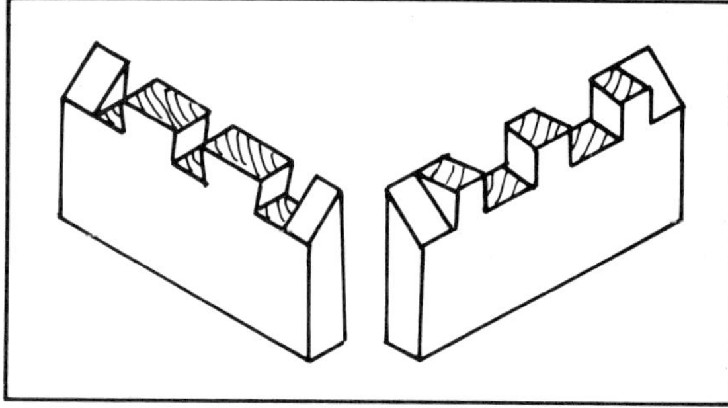

Figure 133 *Through dovetail with mitres*

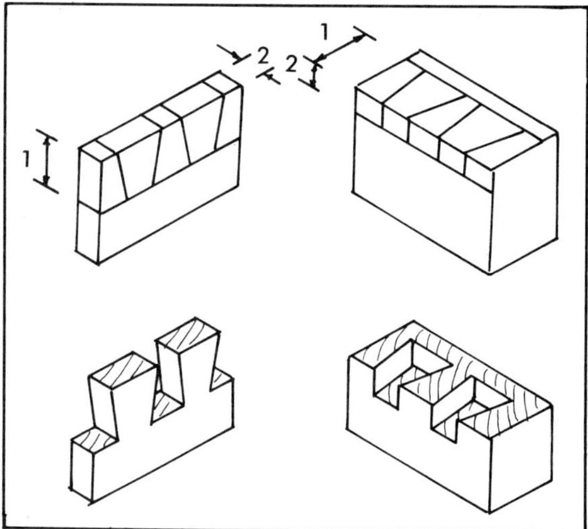

Figure 134 *Lap dovetail*

the amount to be mitred and gauge along the edge from cut-line to cut-line. Mark out the dovetails between the mitres in the normal way. Cut out the pins but leave the mitres for now. Mark out the pins on the second half of the joint and remove the waste.

Before the joint can be fitted the mitres must be worked. With a sliding bevel set to 45 degrees mark the mitres on the edges of the wood. Check carefully that they are the right way round. Arrange the four pieces of wood in box order and it will then be easy to check the mitres. Look at figure 133 which shows some mitres and then saw off the waste. Notice that in the right hand piece the saw cut down the grain is only at 45 degrees not right through like the first part. Finish off the mitres with a chisel and check each one with the sliding bevel. Now the joint can be fitted.

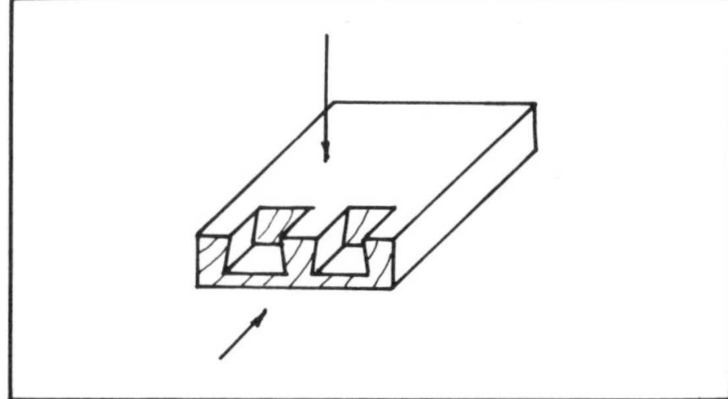

Figure 135 *Lap dovetail pins*

Lap dovetails

In this joint one half is hidden, which makes it suitable for drawer fronts. No joints will show until the drawer is pulled out. Since this is the only time the joint is mentioned in this book it will be used as an example.

Study figure 134 which shows the lap dovetail marked out and underneath the completed joint. First, decide the size of the lap, that is, the amount of the end of the drawer front not to be included in the joint. This will be quite large in the case of bow-fronted drawers where the front has to be shaped. 3/16in. (4.8mm) is an average while 1/8in. (3.2mm) is getting to the bare minimum. Because of this lap the drawer front is thicker than the sides.

Marking out

Set a cutting gauge to the thickness of the drawer front, less the amount of lap (see **1** in figure 134) and gauge across the end of the front and the front end of the side. Re-set the gauge to the thickness **2** of the side and gauge the second line on the drawer front.

Making

Make the tails on the drawer side as for through dovetails. Use the same method to mark out the drawer front. Place the drawer front in the vice with the end up. Saw down the sides of the waste with a tenon saw as far as it will go from line to line. Saw this waste out with a coping saw. This will remove about half of the waste. Take the front and 'G' cramp it to the bench and remove the rest of the waste with a chisel and mallet. Chop down first using light taps horizontally because these will be cuts with the grain, whilst the first were across (figure 135). Go right to the limit of the lap but do not, at this stage, attempt to clean the rest of the waste out. Uncramp and put the front in the vice and complete the cleaning out in this position. It gives a clearer view of what is happening and the side can be fitted at the same time. Make sure that the waste at the back up against the lap is all cleared out, or the dovetail will tend to move out and leave gaps.

Figure 136 *Different sized tails*

Variations

It is not necessary to make all the tails the same size. There is room for experiment with the small chest as it has a longer row of dovetails than the average box. Figure 136 shows one possibility where the tails get larger as they come to the centre. This could be more exaggerated or they could be made to change in pairs. It looks quite attractive to have two smaller tails at each end. This has a practical advantage of giving maximum strength where it is required.

DRAWER CONSTRUCTION

The person who can make a perfect fitting drawer is well on the way to becoming a craftsman. A smoothly operating drawer is a pleasure to use, while one that sticks and requires a sharp tug, is a snare to the unwary. To achieve a smooth action requires a clear knowledge of the construction of a drawer and a sound method of attack.

Each drawer must be dealt with individually to allow for problems which may occur during construction.

The cabinet maker will want to use solid wood throughout, so the drawer bottom as well as the sides and front will also be solid wood. In order to do this the grain of the bottom runs from side to side across the drawer. It is glued at intervals to the groove in the drawer front, and allowed to move from the back.

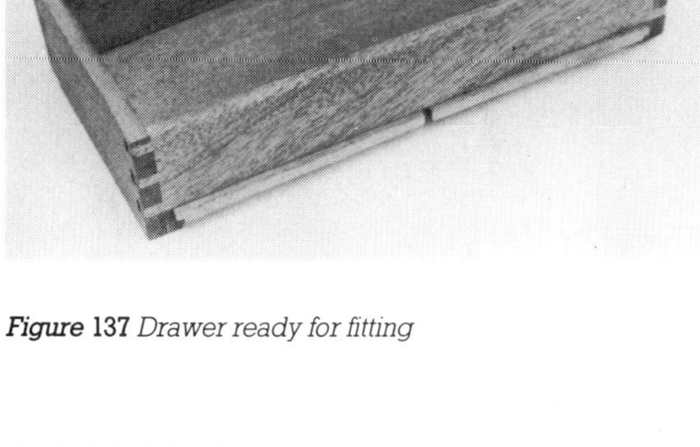

Figure 137 *Drawer ready for fitting*

Study figure 137 which shows a drawer for the small chest in figure 84. It is ready for fitting to its opening. The drawer front is too wide at this stage and the front has still to be shaped. The lap dovetails joining the sides to the front are just visible, while the through dovetails at the back are clearer. A screw will go in the slot and into the drawer back to hold the bottom in place. Notice that the drawer back is set below the sides and the corners of the sides are sloped (figures 138 and 139).

Sides

Do not follow the normal procedure when preparing the sides. Leave the wood a little wider than required and instead of planing down to thickness stop before the gauge line is

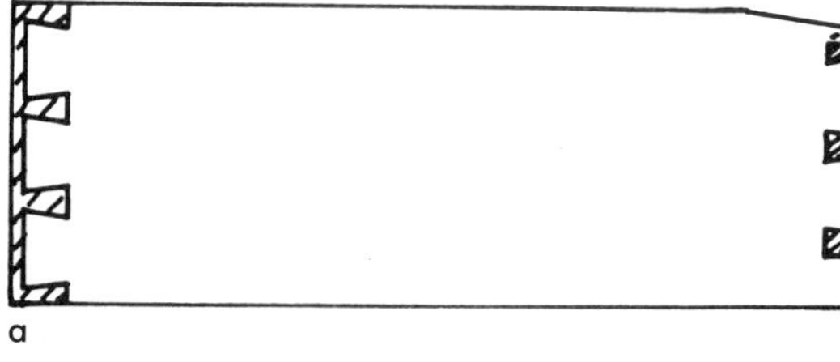

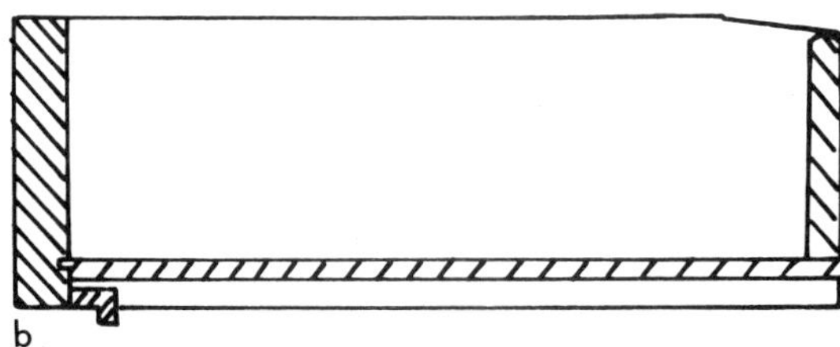

Figure 138 *(a) Side elevation of drawer. (b) Sectional side elevation of drawer including drawer stop.*

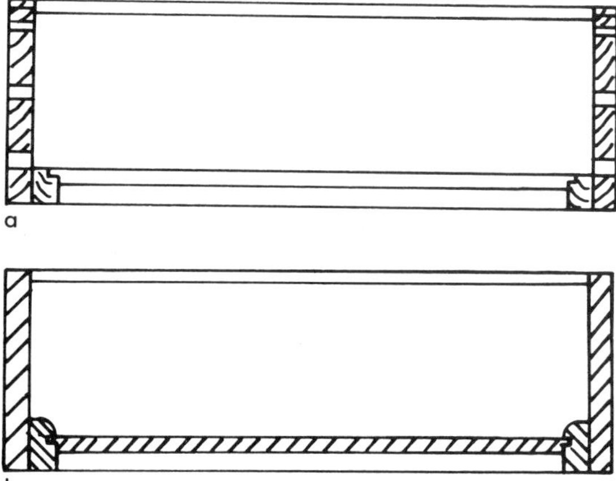

Figure 139 *(a) End elevation of drawer. (b) Sectional end elevation of drawer*

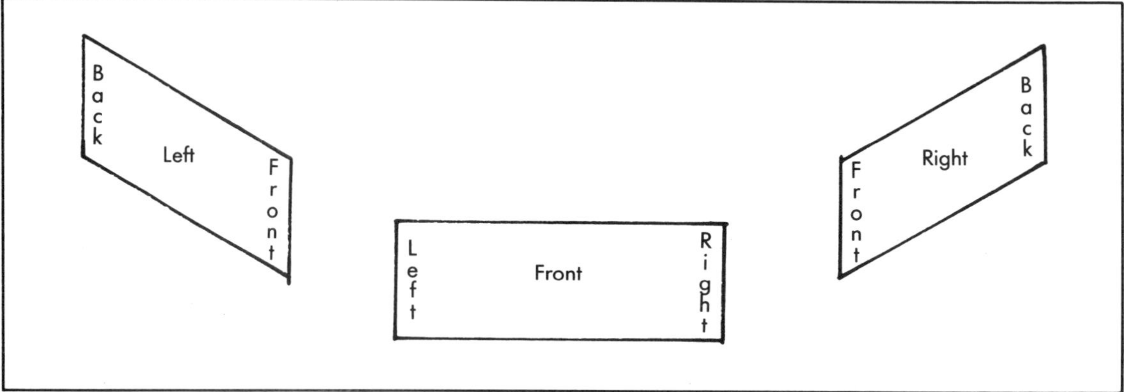

Figure 140 *Preparation of sides*

5 *(Top)* Box veneered with burr walnut and box topped with walnut bark

6 *(Bottom)* Walnut chest and mahogany chest

7 *(Top)* Small turned boxes

8 *(Right)* Circular walnut chest

reached leaving 1/32in. (1mm) to be removed during the cleaning of the drawer after it has been glued. Take one piece and label the outside Right and plane to width at the same time fitting it to the actual drawer opening. Do the same for the Left. Mark the two sides to length with a marking knife. Square these lines all the way round. Saw off the waste and plane the ends. Remembering that the sides are named on the outside with reference to their eventual position in the drawer, mark Front and Back on the ends of the two pieces (figure 140).

Back

The back is narrower than the sides (figure 138). It comes down only as far as the drawer bottom and is also set down at the top to allow the side to be angled off. Work on it until it fits the drawer opening. Mark it Left and Right.

Drawer front

Plane one edge and then make the front one about 1/8in. (3.2mm) wider than the drawer opening. Plane the ends so that the drawer front is the same length as the drawer opening, and the angle of the ends exactly matches each end of the opening. It will not slide in because it is too wide. Mark it Left and Right.

Front joint

This is a conventional lap dovetail. Note that the groove in the drawer front runs behind the bottom tail. This can be seen in figure 138.

Back joint

This is a through dovetail. The general arrangement is shown in figure 138.

Joint

Mark out and make all four joints for the drawer. Fit them carefully.

Front groove

Plough the groove in the drawer front.

Clean up and glue

Clean up and polish all the inside surfaces and then cramp up the drawer. Check the diagonals and make sure that the drawer is out of wind. Should it be in wind each joint will have to be examined individually to see where the trouble lies. The offending joint must be corrected. It is caused at the time the tails are used to mark out the pins if the two pieces are not held at right angles. Do not glue-up until the joints fit correctly.

At this stage the reason for not planing the sides right down to the gauge line is appreciated. The tails are all slightly proud of the pins allowing flat cramping blocks to be used.

Drawer slips

To minimise the weight of the drawer a thinner wood is used for the sides. These would be considerably weakened if a groove was taken out to accommodate the groove on the drawer bottom. To get round this, a strip of wood called a drawer slip is first of all grooved and then glued to the inside of the drawer sides. Figure 141 shows a drawer with one slip glued on and the other slip by the side of it. To show the small tenon on the front end of the slip it has been turned round, effectively hiding the groove which runs along its length. The stub tenon will fit into the groove in the drawer front.

It is difficult to plough a groove in a narrow piece of thin wood like a drawer slip. Take a wide piece of wood, long enough to make several drawer slips, plough the grooves and then saw the slips off. Leave some waste and if the rough edge is left to protrude below the drawer it can be planed-off after the slip has been glued on. Cut into lengths allowing some spare. Make a little tenon on the front of each

Figure 141 *Drawer showing the joint arrangement. One slip is fitted and another is ready*

slip and cut out at the back. round off the top edge and polish.

Before the slip can be glued to the drawer side the polish must be removed from the area to be taken up with the slip. It is easier to remove the polish now than it would have been to have left that part unpolished. Hold a chisel vertically and scrape along the surface. Glue and hold the slips in place with 'G' cramps (figure 142). Plane-off the back corners of the drawer sides.

Drawer bottom

The drawer bottom has a tongue on the front and two ends which fit the grooves in the drawer front and slips (figure 143). Start by planing the bottom to size allowing some extra width. Work the rebates with a shoulder plane or side fillister. Fit the bottom to the drawer so that it will slide easily into place.

The bottom is held in the groove at the front by dabs of glue at intervals. At the rear it is screwed through a slot into the drawer back. Drill the correct clearance hole for the screw and then saw into it. This is shown in figure 143. The result will be to hold the back in place, but allow it to expand and contract as necessary. Clean up the end of the drawer, polish the bottom and then fasten it in place.

Before commencing the next section plane-off the back corners of the drawer sides (figure 138).

***Figure* 142** *Drawer slips glued and cramped*

***Figure* 143** *Underneath the drawer with the bottom partly withdrawn to show the groove in the front and the tongues on the bottom*

Cleaning up and fitting

These two functions are performed at the same time. It is worth remembering how the drawer was made. The sides were planed to fit the drawer opening so that they are already the exact width. The front was planed to the exact length as was the end. Once any surplus has been planed from the bottom of the drawer slips it is only the spare on the thickness of the sides which can prevent the drawer fitting. Use a finely set plane and take off one shaving at a time constantly fitting the drawer into its opening.

Fasten a screw into the position to be taken up by the handle, this will provide something to grip and enable the drawer to be pulled out. The drawer should either fit just proud or slightly set in. The final adjustment is achieved by paring off the front of the drawer stop.

Drawer stop

The drawer stop is shown in figure 138 and is covered in Chapter 8.

13

GLUING AND CRAMPING

A wide choice of adhesive is available today, but each tends to have a specific application. It is essential to use the correct glue or there will be joint failure. There are three important time spans involved in successful gluing.

GLUING

Time spans

1 Assembly time
This is the time that can be allowed after the glue has been applied, during which the pieces of wood can be moved around and adjusted. It becomes increasingly important as the size and complexity of the job increases. Once this time has passed everything must be in its place because the glue will have started to set. This is sometimes called gelling time because some glues start to thicken and the surplus glue can no longer be squeezed out. With other glues the chemical reaction has reached a critical state.

2 Setting time
This is the time during which the cramps must be left on.

3 Full strength
It may well be several days before the full strength of the glue is reached but work can proceed.

General notes
Glue is no substitute for ill-fitting joints. All glues tend to shrink during drying and if there is a gap between the joint the glue will come away from one side.

Because of its cellular construction wood cannot be successfully glued end to end. However side to side it can be glued so securely that any subsequent fracture will occur away from the glue line. The artificial bond is stronger than the natural one. Mitres, because of their likeness to end grain, are also very weak joints and for this reason are frequently strengthened with veneer keys.

PVA glue

The most convenient, readily available glues for wood, are the PVA glues. They come ready prepared in the form of a creamy white liquid. It needs applying only to one half of the joint. Once it comes out of its container it starts to set, so from the first application the work should be together in its final form within ten to fifteen minutes on a warm day. In winter, in an unheated workshop, this could stretch to an hour. Similarly in the summer the cramps can come off after an hour or so but in the winter, under adverse conditions, it could take overnight or even 24 hours for the glue to set.

Resin glue

This is a very different glue which consists of a glue and a hardener. The glue comes in the form of a white powder, which is added to water to make a white syrup, and a colourless liquid which is the hardener. No setting can take place until both the glue and the hardener come into contact. The glue is applied to one half of the joint and the hardener to the other. This has a great advantage since it means that the glue and hardener can be applied but the assembly time does not start until the first joint is put together and glue meets hardener. The assembly time is 15 minutes. This considerably extends the time which is available and is essential with a complicated construction. Under normal conditions the cramps can come off in three hours. Once again temperature plays a part in these times. Although it not relevant to the work in this book it is worth remembering that this glue is waterproof.

Animal glue

Scotch or animal glue is required for veneering because of its particular qualities. One of these is its more or less instant 'tack'. This means that if two pieces of wood are glued and brought together there is an instant tendency to stick. The other quality is the way in which it can be melted by the application of heat. These qualities are very important to anyone wanting to veneer. Full details of the preparation are given in the section on veneering.

Latex glue

This is a rubber-based glue which comes ready prepared. It will glue cloth to wood and make a flexible bond. This makes it very suitable for tambours. It is a very clean glue and any surplus can be rubbed off, leaving a clean surface. To prevent a tendency to penetrate a fabric, lightly spread a layer of glue on both surfaces and allow the glue to dry. This will take about 15 minutes. Bring the two surfaces together and a firm bond will result.

Epoxy resin

A two part glue for gluing metal.

CRAMPING

It is essential that any joints are pulled up tight and held like that until the glue is dry. This requires some form of cramping. This can vary from tightly wound string to an elaborate arrangement of cramps. Since cramps are expensive items it is worth making a simple form of cramp which will hold a box together until the glue is dry.

Figure 144 shows this sort of cramp in use. It is made of strips of metal, bolts and wing nuts. Using 2in. (50mm) bolts allows a reasonable range of different sized boxes to be cramped-up. This length may be increased as required. The right angle bends can be accurately made by hammering the strips over a block of wood. If wing nuts are used it will obviate the use of a spanner. This method of cramping is particularly useful for mitred constructions. By using more than four strips and altering the angles this type of cramp can be used on boxes with more than four sides.

Types of cramps

There are two types of cramps which will be useful, 'G' and sash cramps (figures 142 and 145). It is useful to buy four sash cramps, since they are often used in fours. For the work in this book it is best to buy 2ft cramps. While the price does not rise much for longer ones, a cramp which is longer than necessary is difficult to use and its sheer weight can be a disadvantage. To start with, two 6in. 'G' cramps should be sufficient. As well as holding things together they will also hold a piece of wood on the bench while it is worked on.

Cramping butt-mitres

The sequence of operations required to glue-up a butt-mitred box is shown in a sequence of photographs (figure 145a, b and c). First secure the long sides in cramps having carefully lined them up so that they are held in line with the bar of the cramp. (The photograph shows the two mitred ends ready to be glued in.) Make sure that they are vertical and avoid excess pressure which will damage the mitres. Arrange the cramps the correct distance apart so that the ends can be slotted into position. Glue the ends and slide them in to place. Put another pair of cramps across the box as seen in figure 145b, the edges of the cramps right up to the corners. With care the original pair of cramps can be moved slightly inwards so that they too occupy a position with their outside edges in line with the corners. This final arrangement is shown in figure 145c. For the first time at least, go through the operation without glue until familiar with the sequence of moves. Check the diagonals and also for wind.

Figure **144** *The homemade cramps in use on a butt-mitred box of walnut. The completed box appears in figure 50*

Figure **145a** *Cramping-up a butt-mitred box. The two sides held in sash cramps. The ends can be seen in the foreground*

Figure **145b** *Cramping-up a butt-mitred box. The ends have been dropped in place and two cramps added*

Figure **145c** *Cramping-up a butt-mitred box. The cramps are carefully re-arranged to line up with the corners of the box*

Testing

Once the cramps are in position it is essential that two tests are made. The first is to see that the box is square, that is that the angles are all right-angles. This is done by measuring the diagonals. If they are equal then the box is square. If they are not then the cramps have to be adjusted until they are. Follow the rule which states that 'the cramps must be moved in the direction of the long diagonal'. Figure 146 makes this clear. After adjustment measure the diagonals again. Continue until the two diagonals are exactly the same. A steel ruler is useful for measuring, or a piece of wood with a flat end which will fit into a corner may also be used and the length of the diagonal marked with a pencil. This can then be used for the second diagonal and the two pencil marks compared. If they are different the true length is half-way between the two marks.

A second test must be made to see that the box is not twisted or in wind. Look across the top of the box; the sides should be in line with each other. Rest a piece of waste wood on one of the corners which is sticking up and tap lightly with a hammer.

Cramping dovetails

In some ways cramping a dovetailed box is easier than a mitred one, since the joints already hold the sides and ends together. All that is needed is a way in which they can be tightly closed up and held like that until the glue is dry. There is one complication, the pressure must be directed onto the tails and these may be level

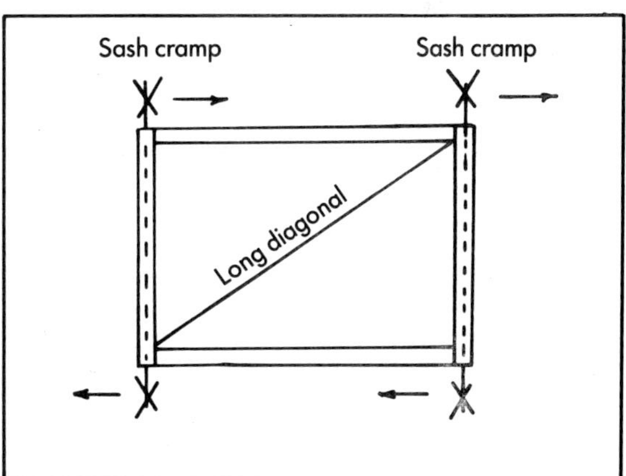

Figure **146** *Test for squareness*

***Figure* 147** *Cramping blocks. From back to front. Sloping sides and ends. Dovetails. Sloping dovetails*

***Figure* 148** *Bow-fronted small chest in S American mahogany. The first cramping of the two shelves. Note the slot ready for the drawer stop*

with or even below the pins. If this is the case, cramping blocks must be made to fit over the pins. A pair of these specially shaped cramping blocks are shown in the middle of figure 147. They were used to cramp-up the small chest and are shown in action in figure 149. These blocks have to be individually made to suit the work being glued-up.

With forethought this problem can be tackled in another way. This is normal practice in drawer construction (see Chapter 12). If the sides of the box are not planed down to their finished thickness but left too thick and put together like this the tails will stick above the pins. In this case a flat cramping block can be used stretching right across and the extra thickness planed-off after the glue is dry.

Cramp-up the box dry to check the joints before actually gluing. As the boxes get larger then the number of cramps being used must be increased. Sloping cramping blocks are used to glue-up a dovetailed box with sloping sides.

The same test as described for butt-mitres must be made, that is the diagonals must be checked and the box examined for wind.

Cramping chests

If a number of pieces have to be glued-up, requiring pressure in different areas it is easier and more satisfactory to do the gluing-up in a series of operations. The carcase of a chest is just such an example. First of all glue in the shelves (figure 148). Rest two sash cramps across the bench and place the chest on it (the two sides and the two shelves). Put two pieces of wood against each end. These should stretch across the two shelves. Four separate strips could be used, but this is rather more troublesome. Add two cramps across the top and tighten up. Proceed by checking the diagonals and check also for wind.

***Figure* 149** *The second cramping-up, this time the dovetail joints. Note the incomplete shaping of the two sides*

When the glue is dry uncramp and clean off any excess. Now glue the top and bottom. Put three cramps across the bench and use the specially prepared cramping blocks. Three cramps are required to make sure that the joints come up in the middle as well as at the ends. Add three more cramps across the top (figure 149).

If only four cramps are available use deeper cramping blocks to transmit the pressure more effectively.

Make the usual tests.

Cramping blocks

These are very important. Make sure that the side of the block which comes in to contact with the box or chest is planed accurately. If a rough piece is used it could leave unsightly marks which are difficult to remove.

The cramping blocks at the top of figure 147 were used to cramp up the box shown in figure 35 where sides and ends sloped. In order that the cramps could pull up squarely, these blocks were made with tapered strips pinned onto shaped pieces of plywood. Loose pieces would have been impossible to control. The cramping blocks in the foreground were used on the box shown in figure 31.

14

CLEANING UP AND POLISHING

CLEANING UP

Cleaning up is a vital stage in the whole polishing process. If this stage is skimped no amount of effort later will compensate and the final result will be unsatisfactory. Using the minimum tool kit this can be done with a jack plane, but if the box is only small it would be easier with a smoothing plane. In either case the first thing to do is to sharpen the plane.

Plane setting

After the blade has been sharpened, set the cap iron to within 1⁄16in. (1.6mm) of the end of the blade. At the same time advance the frog of the plane so that the mouth will be narrower. Slacken the two bolts which hold the frog down (figure 150), and then turn the screw at the back of the frog in a clockwise direction. Tighten the securing bolts, put the blade in position and fasten it with the lever cap. Test the plane on a piece of waste wood. It should plane almost any grain, however difficult. (When the plane is required for rougher work the adjustments must be made in reverse.) In some cases it may be necessary to plane across the grain in order to stop it tearing.

Glass paper

Do as little glasspapering as possible. A planed surface is to be preferred if it is really smooth. Using highly figured wood it will be necessary to finish with glass paper. Work down to a fine grade like no. 0 or Flour paper. Use a cork block and this will help to stop the corners being rounded off. It will also help to avoid local hollows where there is a particularly difficult spot. Glass paper is graded according to its roughness. The grades working from fine to rough are:

Flour	0	1	1½	F2
240	220	150	120	100

The figures underneath are the new system which is gradually coming in using grit sizes. If the surface is dampened and re-glasspapered a smoother surface will result.

Cleaning up a butt-mitred box

Start with the sides, holding the box in the vice. Since there is no end grain to worry about it is only necessary to be sure to plane with the grain. Take off as little wood as possible in even layers across the surface. Work right round the box.

***Figure* 150** *A jack plane showing the frog and adjusting screws. The cap iron and blade are in the foreground*

Cleaning up the top and bottom edges is more difficult. Hold the wood in the vice with the top edges uppermost. Rest the plane across from edge to edge and work in a circular movement round the corners, always resting the plane on two, preferably opposite, edges. Doing it like this will keep the edges in the horizontal plane and stop them from rounding off. Use the edge of a steel ruler on each edge and also look across to see that the edges are out of wind.

Cleaning up a dovetailed box

Start on the sides with the box held in the vice. Do not plane from one end to the other, or the end grain presented by the dovetail pins or tails will split. Check the grain direction and plane against the grain for about 1in. (25mm), just to get clear of the end grain. Now plane with the grain stopping at the area already planed. Repeat for the other three faces. The top is the same as for the butt-mitre.

Cleaning up before gluing

Before gluing, clean up and polish any parts which would be difficult or impossible to polish afterwards, for example, the inside of boxes and any panel before it is fixed in its groove. This polishing has the added advantage of making it easier to remove any surplus glue after gluing-up, since glue will not stick to a waxed surface.

POLISHING

It is very difficult, if not impossible, to find a finish which enhances the beauty of wood in quite the same way as beeswax. It helps to bring out the grain and the colour. It has another quality, the more it is rubbed the better it shines. A lot of finishes gradually deteriorate as the years pass but, with an occasional re-waxing, a patina is gradually built up which will only improve the look of the work. Its disadvantage, if that is the right word, is that it will show up clearly every defect in the wood and every rough patch that has not been properly cleaned up.

Wax polish

If necessary the polish can be made by shredding beeswax and covering it with turpentine, then heating it in a double saucepan. Great care should be taken, and on no account must the mixture be allowed near a naked fame or heated directly. The result is a rather soft polish so it is perhaps better to obtain a proprietry brand. These usually have an additive, which makes for a harder and tougher finish and a solvent which evaporates more quickly than turpentine. Choose a neutral coloured polish otherwise it will change the colour of the wood. The makers instructions are to use as sparingly as possible or there will be a build up of wax which will attract dust.

Preparation for wax

Assuming the surface has been cleaned up and glasspapered, it helps if the grain is filled with a coat of diluted bleached shellac. This is sold as pale or extra pale polish. Dilute this half and half with methylated spirit, apply an even coat and rub it in until it is dry. Go over the surface with flour paper. Do not use a cork block because, as the polish is taken off, it will tend to build up in patches on the glass paper which will scratch the wood. Using fingers only, these patches can be avoided. It will only need gentle treatment and care must be exercised near the edges. Continue until any shellac remaining on the surface has been removed, leaving a very smooth surface. If in doubt when to stop glasspapering, hold the work up to the light and if it glints there is still polish to remove. The surface should have a flat smooth look.

Applying wax

This is the easy part and only if the preliminary stages have been attended to will it be successful. Using a lint free cloth apply a small amount of wax and leave for half an hour or so to allow the solvent to evaporate. Now rub and a lovely shine will be the result.

Polyurethane varnish

This is less attractive but more durable. It can be obtained in either a gloss or matt finish. It also comes in an almost colourless form or with various colours added. It is ideal for boxes which are likely to be subject to very hard wear, for example childrens playboxes or boxes for storage in the workshop. When the wood has been prepared brush on an even coat, trying not to overlap brush strokes. Use a light pressure and as little brushing as possible. Let this coat dry, which may take 24 hours. Rub over the surface with very fine wire wool, '0' or '00' grade to remove any rough patches. Glass paper can be used but the wire wool will be found to be better because it does not clog like glass paper. Brush off any dust and give a second coat.

Combined wax and polyurethane varnish

In this method the varnish is used as the sealer. Brush on an even coat and allow to dry hard. Rub right down to the wood with wire wool. If the wood has a very open grain this can be repeated. Now rub on the wax as for wax polishing. This method has some of the advantages of both finishes.

15

FITTINGS

HINGEING

Brass hinges

Figure 151 shows a selection of hinges. The first is the best quality, made from solid brass with the hole for the pin drilled out. This type is called a solid-drawn brass butt-hinge and it is ordered by its length and width. There are two widths, which are referred to as broad or narrow suite. The others are lightweight leaf hinges, in which the thin brass is bent round to form the pin hole. This type is not as strong as the solid variety.

The instructions for fitting these hinges will refer to particular measurements; they are shown at the top of figure 152. **l** is the length of the hinge, **w** is the width measuring from the centre of the pin, **t** is the thickness when the leaves of the hinge are parallel, and half **t**. (This is important when dealing with leaf hinges.)

Flat lid

This applies to lids which are effectively just flat pieces of wood which may or may not be clamped or framed. Look at detail **a** and **b** in figure 152. In the first case the hinge is sunk entirely into the box, whilst in **b** the hinge is half way into the top and half way into the box. For flat lids the first method is adopted.

Mark the position of the hinge on the back edge of the box. Hinges 1in. (25mm) long and over, set their own length in from the box edge. Shorter hinges should be set in 1in. (25mm). Square across the top edge and a short distance down each side with a pencil. Set a marking gauge to **t** and gauge between the pencil lines. If the hinge is narrower than the thickness of the wood then the marking gauge must be used to mark this measurement **w** as shown in figure 152.

If the hinge stretches right across, saw on the waste side of the lines down to the gauge line amd make three more cuts in between. This will help prevent any splitting ahead of the chisel during the next stage. Chisel down to the line. Do not go below the line since this will cause difficulties. See 'faults' further on.

If the hinge is narrower than the wood, only that part occupied by the hinge is removed. Instead of sawing right across, saw at an angle and use a chisel to complete the cut. Then chisel out the waste being careful not to go right across.

Check the fit of the hinge and test with the

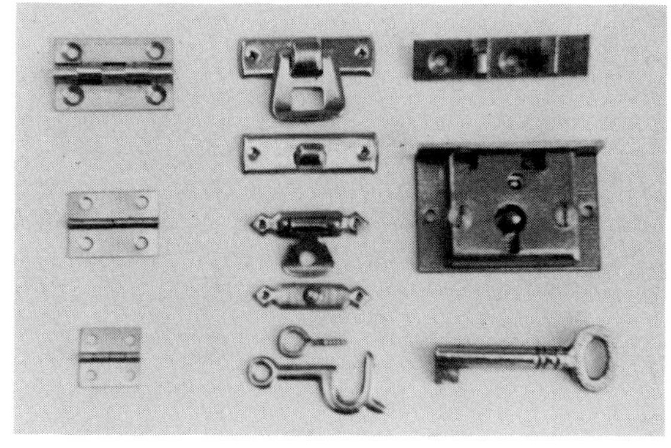

Figure 151 *In the left column a selection of hinges. In the middle a variety of catches. On the right a box lock*

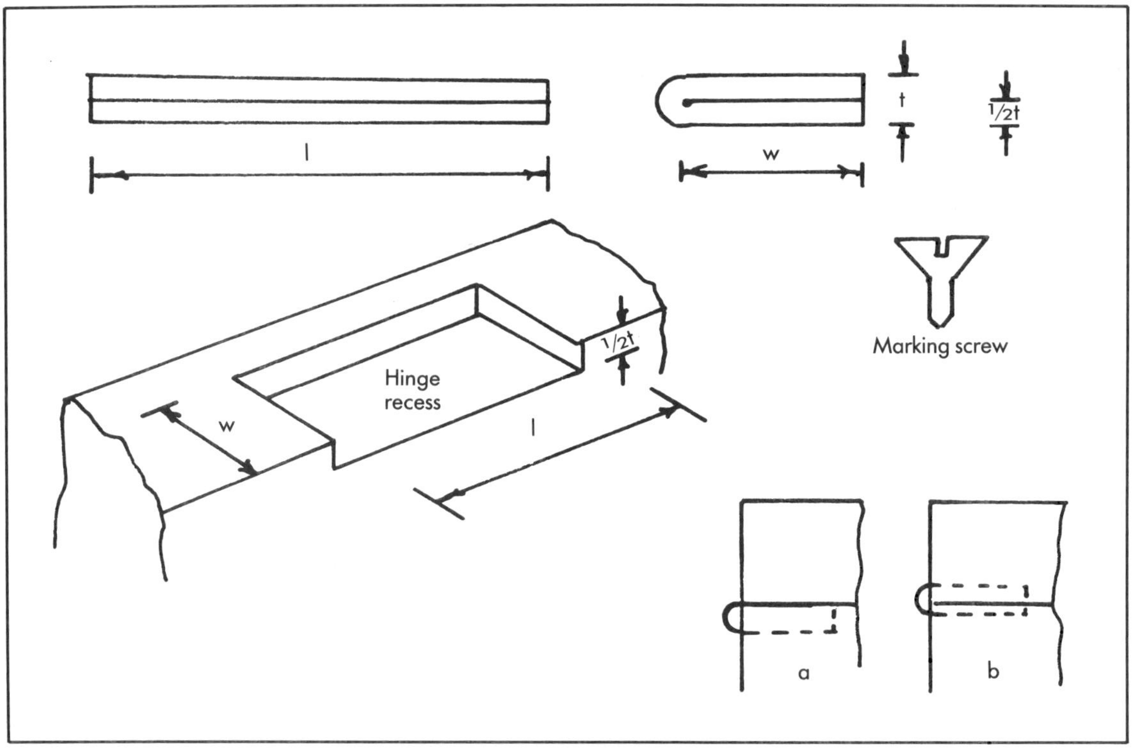

Hinge recess

Marking screw

Figure 152 *Solid-drawn brass-butt hinge*

Figure 153 *Holding the lid of the rosewood treasure chest together, while the hinges are fitted using a sash cramp*

edge of a steel ruler that it comes just level with the top of the box. Screw the hinges in place with the centre of the pin of the hinge in line with the edge of the box. Mark the centre of each hole and pre-drill. A convenient drill can be made by taking a panel pin and nipping off the end with a pair of pliers and using this as a drill. A little wax on the thread of the screws will help to stop the screws breaking off when they are tightened.

Take a number of screws equal to that required to complete the hingeing. These can be steel so long as they fit the holes in the hinges. File them down as shown in figure 152. Clamp the head between two pieces of wood with the thread sticking out and hold them in the vice. File down until, when the are placed in the remaining holes and the hinge is shut, the points stick out. These are the markers which will enable the top to be perfectly lined up. With these markers in place, press the top down. This will indicate where the screws should go in the top. Pre-drill these holes in the same way as the first ones and screw a screw in each hole and then take it out. Now the top can be screwed into place quite easily. It should line up perfectly.

Note. The small brass screws required for these small hinges are very delicate. Use a screw driver that accurately fits the slot in the head, always pre-drill and use wax on the thread. In oak, use a steel screw before introducing the brass ones. If the screw breaks off it will have to be chopped out and the hole filled before work can proceed.

Figure 154 *Lock fitted to walnut writing box*

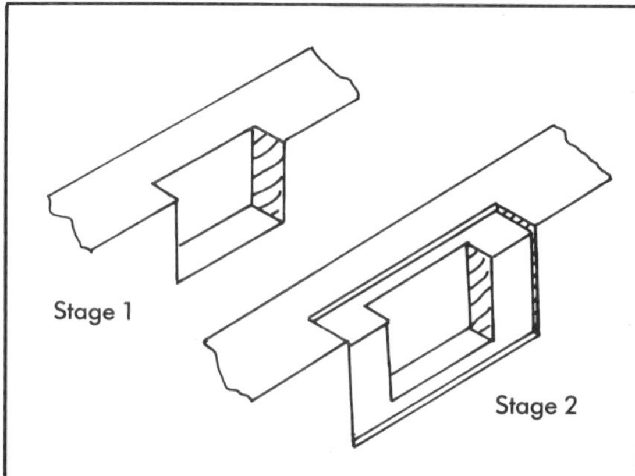

Figure 155 *Recess for drawer lock*

Sawn off lids

These types of lid require a slightly different technique and the hinges are set equally into the top and the bottom. Cramp the top alongside the box (figure 153). The lid is packed up until it is level with the bottom. Square across both edges, remove from the cramp and continue as before using the measurement '½t'.

When the hinge recesses have been cut, re-cramp and fit the hinges aiming at a tight fit. The centre of the hinge must run exactly in line with the edge of the box. Mark the centres of the holes and pre-drill and screw the hinges in position. Shut the lid and check the line up. If there is a slight discrepancy a bradawl can be used to re-direct the screws. If the discrepancy is large, plug the holes and start again. If the hinge has three holes, start with two until everything is all right and then complete the screwing. If the lid will not close it may be a clash of screw heads. If they are too big change them, if they go in at an angle straighten them up.

If the screws are correct then the hinges may have been sunk in too far. This means unscrewing the hinges and planing down the top edge of the box and, if the hinge is set into the lid, this as well.

A gap at the back of the box means setting the hinges lower.

CATCHES

There is not a great variety of catches to choose from (figure 151). The side hook is the easiest to come by and it is available in a range of sizes. It consists of a hook screwed into place and a screw eye for it to slide into. Screw the hook into place. Careful placing of the screw eye will keep the box tightly closed. Pre-drill for the screw and the screw eye. The latter is particularly fragile.

The other catches are designed to be held in place with brass pins. A better solution is to use small brass screws, enlarging the holes in the catches if this is necessary. In figure 52 one of these catches is in place on a rosewood box. Screws have been used and it is doubtful if brass pins could have been driven into such hard wood.

LOCKS

The lock in figure 151 is 1½in. (38mm) long and is the smallest quality lock on the market. This is far too big and cumbersome for most of the work in this book. However, one this size is fitted to the writing box in figure 154 but the side had to be specially thickened to take it. It requires wood at least ½in. (12mm) thick.

To fit this lock, first mark out the position of the key hole. Square a line with a pencil down the centre front of the box. Set a marking gauge against the lock and set it to the distance from the top to the centre of the steel pin. Gauge across the pencil line and drill a hole ¼in. (6mm) deep. Hold the lock in place on the inside of the box and scribe round it. Figure 155 shows the wood to be removed. Follow up with the second stage. The lock should fit snugly in place, flush along the top and the inside.

Complete the keyhole by drilling a smaller hole at the lower limit of the slot. Joint the two holes. A penknife may come in handy here.

Screw the lock in place and lock the top catch in place. Close the lid and press down firmly. The two studs will clearly mark its position on the lid of the box. Open the lid, unlock the top part and let this into the top. Screw it in place and test the operation of the lock. The position of the top is very critical and, if the lock will not close, a little filing may be necessary.

There is a slightly smaller lock measuring 1¾in. (32mm) long and only 3⁄16in. (4.8mm) thick which would fit into sides ⅜in. (10mm) thick. However, it is a very light lock and compares in quality as a leaf hinge with a solid drawn one.

MUSICAL MOVEMENTS

The fitting of a musical movement to a box changes it from the ordinary to something special. A wide variety of tunes is available. Holding the movement by hand the sound is barely audible, but surrounded by wood it is greatly magnified.

The movements are wound by a key on a shaft passing through the bottom of the box. This key has to be free to turn and have some movement up and down. This means allowing sufficient diameter and depth. Either the handle can protrude clear of the bottom, in which case feet must be added to give clearance for the key, or the bottom can be thick enough to allow the key to be inset into a circular recess (figure 156).

Before the box is designed, choose the movement and measure it up. If the handle is to be recessed it will mean quite a thick bottom, which suggests rebating it so that some of the thickness is disguised

If the handle is to turn below the bottom, then plywood can be used, but in this case it will need some packing under the movement (figure 157). This will take up some of the length of the driving shaft and be better able to take the securings screws.

Figure 157 shows the gradual building-up of the sounding box. The sides end ends are butt jointed and glued. The top can either be made to push tightly into place or just spot glued. Either way will allow access to the movement if it is required.

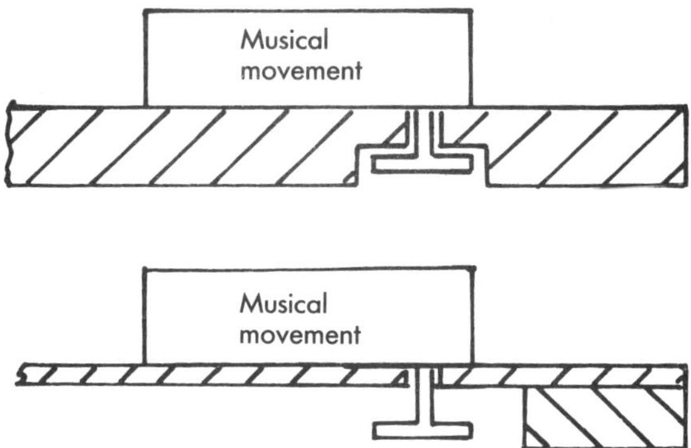

***Figure* 156** *Fitting of handle to musical movement*

***Figure* 157** *Musical movement in place with cover nearly made. Notice the operating wire ready to be cut to length*

The movement is operated by opening the lid and releasing the pressure from the stop wire. The connection between the stop wire and the lid is a straight piece of wire with a loop on the end (figure 157). Drill a hole at an angle through the side of the box to emerge inside the musical compartment. The loop has to be made after the wire is in position, unless the bottom can be removed, in which case it can be fed in from the bottom upwards.

The difficult part comes in deciding how much of the wire should protrude through the side. This is a matter for experience and trial and error. Too short and it will not work, too long and the lid will stick up. It is not a big job to replace it if too much is removed. Figure 158 shows the completed musical box installation.

***Figure* 158** *The completed musical box installation*

When everything is assembled the movement should start when the lid is raised and stop when the lid is closed pressing down on the stop wire. *Note.* The stop wire on the movement may be too long and require shortening. The end which stops the movement by preventing the governor from turning, may need adjustment, since the difference between 'go' and 'no go' is very slight indeed. However, once these movements are set up, they run happily without any further attention.

16

VENEERING, MARQUETRY AND PARQUETRY

VENEERING

Veneering means gluing a thin slice or veneer of wood on to a suitable base. The veneer has usually been taken from a log with a specially attractive grain or from a wood which would be too expensive to use in the solid. Some woods, particularly burrs, are unsuitable in the solid because they lack strength. They are used as veneers because strength is not important in a veneer which is to be glued on to a firm base.

Veneers are made by cutting thin slices of a prepared flitch of the selected timber. Using accurate, sharp knives means that there is little or no waste. The veneer thickness is measured in hundredths of an inch. Some timbers do not slice satisfactorily and they must be sawn. This, in contrast, is very wasteful and therefore expensive.

Most veneers lie flat and these are the ones to practise on. Generally speaking the more exotic the grain, e.g. burrs, the less likely this is to be so. These veneers have bulges in them and they need treatment before they can be laid. Leave them between dampened sheets of newspaper, lightly weighted, for twelve hours or so.

Preparation of base

First of all make the shell of a box using a mitred construction. Glue a piece of plywood across the top and bottom. Cut the plywood slightly over size and plane off the surplus when the glue is dry. Alternatively make a mitred box with rebates top and bottom and glue the plywood in the rebates.

Note that the surface must always be sound, free from knots, shakes or other flaws, or the veneer cannot be successfully glued to it.

Toothing plane

A toothing plane has a serrated blade held upright and, when this is worked in a figure of eight over the surface, it leaves a slightly roughened surface which helps the gluing. A worn out machine hacksaw blade can be used with a similar effect and without the expense of a toothing plane.

Glue

There is not doubt that old fashioned animal glue, applied hot, is best for veneering. It does, however, require careful preparation. For this a proper glue pot or some form of double saucepan (like a porridge pan) is necessary. The glue can be purchased in the form of pearls. Place them in the inner container and cover them with water. Half fill the outer container with clean water and place over a heater or gas burner. The double saucepan is required to avoid over heating the glue which will quickly degrade if boiled. When the glue has dissolved, test its thickness by letting it run off the brush. It should flow easily off, not too thick and not too thin. The usual mistake is to use the glue when it is too thick.

Sizing

Take some of the prepared glue and dilute it to half strength with hot water and apply a coat to all the surfaces to be veneered. This will act as a partial seal and prevent the glue from soaking into the box leaving nothing on the surface to hold the veneer in place. Leave this to dry overnight.

Veneering

The simplest method and the easiest to apply consists of a single sheet of veneer which is large enough to contain the five pieces required to cover the box. To start with choose a nice flat veneer. Cut the pieces about ¼in. (6mm) larger than required. Use the edge of a steel ruler and a Stanley knife, taking great care when working across the grain to prevent the veneer from tearing. Make a number of light cuts rather than attempting to cut through with one cut.

Start with the two ends, followed by the two sides, leaving the top until last. A warm iron is necessary at this stage. An old electric one is best.

Apply glue to the veneer and the box. Press the veneer into place. Brush a little water on the veneer to stop a tendency to curl, and soften the glue with a warm iron. This will enable any excess glue to be squeezed out with the veneering hammer (see Chapter 10). On a larger area work from the centre outwards working one strip at a time.

When the two ends have been veneered leave them overnight to dry. Clean off the surplus veneer with the knife. Test the veneering by working over the surface tapping with the blunt end of a pencil. A hollow sound will denote an unglued area. Moisten the area and press with a warm iron which will melt the glue and allow the veneer to be pressed into place with the veneering hammer. (Figure 159 shows the work in progress.)

Continue until the box is finished. Clean up and polish. Be very careful using glass paper that it does not penetrate the veneer, especially at the corners. The use of a cork block will help to avoid this problem. (Figure 160 shows a completed box. Note the delicate handle, details in figure 161.)

Two matching pieces

Two consecutive sheets of veneer can produce an attractive pattern when glued together (figure 162). Because the area to be covered is unlikely to be large, the length of the join will be quite short. It should be possible to cut two straight edges. Push the two pieces of veneer tightly together to test the join. This should be perfect. If this method does not work, place the two pieces together between two pieces of wood and, while they are supported like this, plane them. If possible hold them in a vice. If they are too large for this rest them on the bench top and use the plane sliding on its side on the bench (figure 163).

***Figure* 159** *Two sides of the box already veneered and ready for cleaning up. Note the scratched surface of top awaiting veneer*

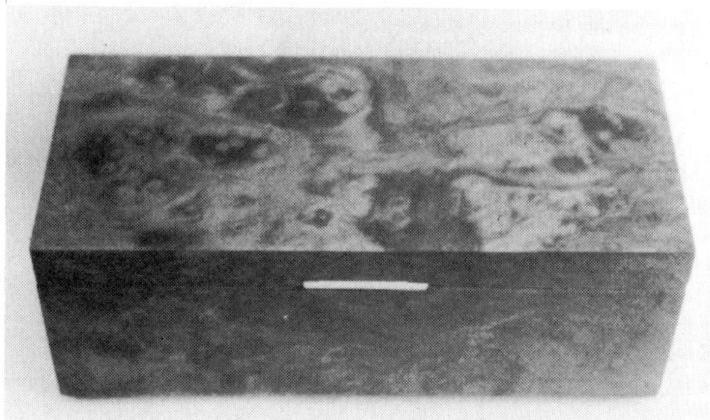

***Figure* 160** *Veneered box with sycamore handle*

***Figure* 161** *Sycamore handle ready to slide into position in its dovetail housing*

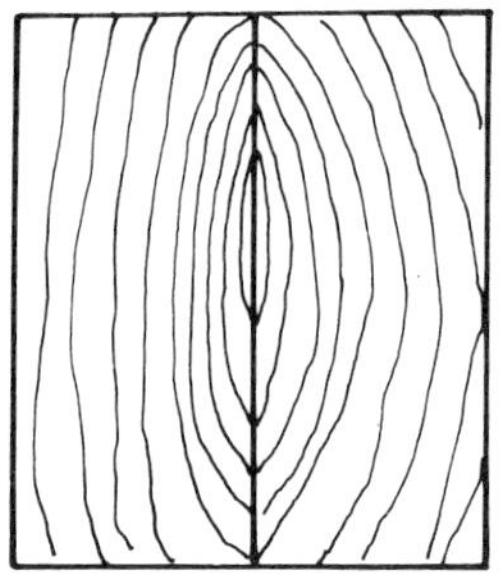
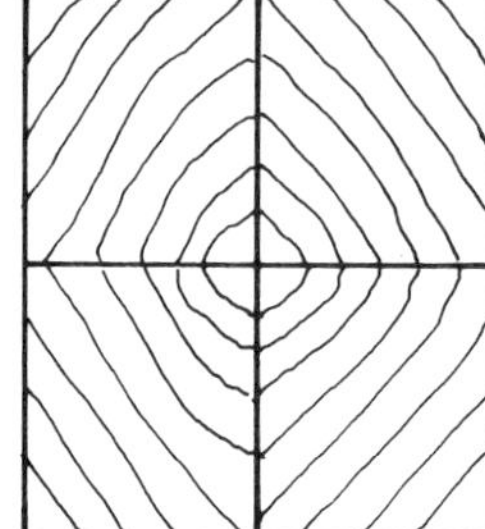

Figure 162 *Veneer designs*

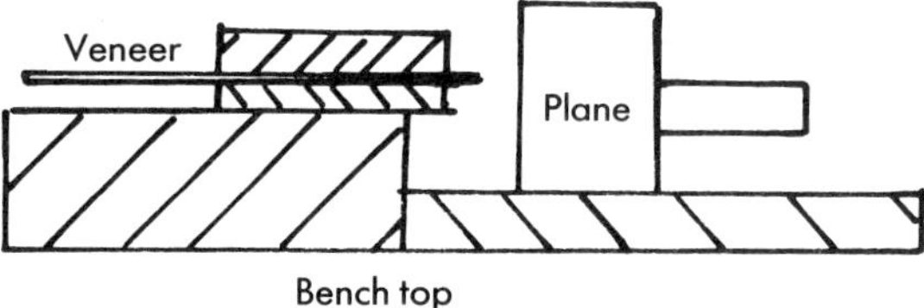

Figure 163 *Planing veneer edges*

Draw a centre line down the surface to be veneered and using the same method used for a single piece of veneer, glue on one half. Settle it in place with the warm iron. Now glue the second half of the box and the second piece of veneer and lay that. Stick a piece of sticky brown paper over the join. Sellotape can be used but it is not as good for this purpose. When the glue is dry the sticky brown paper will peel off if it is dampened and left for a while.

Matching four

Veneer manufacturers go to great lengths to keep the sheets in the order in which they come off the flitch. To make this pattern, four consecutive sheets are needed. The method is similar to that used for two pieces. This time a cross has to be marked out on the top. More difficult the veneer has to fit end-to-end, as well as side-by-side. The results are very satisfying. Figure 162 gives an idea of the sort of pattern which can be achieved.

Cross banding

Cross banding is the traditional way of forming a border round a central panel of veneer. It is called cross banding because the grain runs across the width of the veneer rather than along the length. When the central panel is in place trim the edges back to size with a knife and steel ruler. An iron may be necessary to soften the glue to enable the waste bits of veneer to be pulled off. Cut the strips of cross banding, which can be taken from the same or another veneer, mitre the corners and glue in place. Some brown sticky paper will help. Work all the way round and trim off when the glue is dry.

Banding

See figure 38. A fine strip of contrasting veneer about 1/16in. (1.5mm) looks very attractive between the central panel and the cross banding if the area to be veneered is large enough to take it. With care, working on a fairly small top, the central panel, the banding and the cross banding, can be laid together. (A warm workshop on a hot summers day is desirable.) If this is impossible the narrow banding can be held in place with panel pins and the cross banding added later.

MARQUETRY

General

Marquetry is the art of making pictures in wood. Instead of paint the artist uses small pieces of veneer. Whilst this does not provide the full range of the artist's palette (blue is one of the missing colours) it still leaves plenty of scope. The woods will have different characteristics: the grain may be open or closed; the light will reflect in different ways on different veneers; the same veneer can be turned through 90 or 180 degrees giving quite a different result; some veneers are quite plain, whilst others have exotic patterns with great variety within a small area. Given a wide selection to choose from the craftsman will not find himself limited.

Supply

The first essential is to obtain a good supply of suitable veneers. One way is to visit a stockist and select a number of pieces or to buy one or other of the made-up packs which are sold for this purpose. Another method is to find a manufacturer using decorative veneers in bulk and to see if he has any off-cuts to sell. This will be the cheapest way of building up a stock.

The picture

There is no easy way to success and only experience will make a good marquetarian. If a very difficult picture is chosen for the first attempt the result will be disappointing and very off-putting. Start with a simple picture which has a preponderance of straight lines. Houses are always good subjects and look attractive when they are finished. The ideal way is to find an attractive subject and then to draw it as it is. Using this drawing take out the unnecessary detail and end up with a very simplified version. Instead of attempting clouds, for example, choose a suitable veneer which will suggest a cloudy sky. There are many sources of inspiration and calendars, postcards and holidays brochures are all very useful. The theme for the design used to illustrate this section was taken from a menu. It was turned round and the two parts drawn together to give a mirror image and to change the shape from a rather narrow vertical one to a horizontal one.

Cutting

Before attempting a picture try cutting various shapes out of some waste veneer. A surgical blade held in a holder makes a very good instrument. The blades can be bought from a chemist. Hold the blade as vertically as possible so that adjacent pieces will fit snugly together without a V-shaped gap.

Start cutting with the grain using a steel ruler as a guide. Even with simple lines like this, it will be found that there is a right way as well as a wrong one. In one direction the veneer will tend to split ahead of the knife into the piece that is required, whilst if the cut is made in the opposite direction the splitting, if it occurs, will come in the waste (figure 164).

Now try across the grain but release the pressure as the near edge is reached otherwise it will tend to split down the grain. It is unwise to try to get through the thickness of the veneer in one attempt. The difficulty increases with certain varieties, for example, a very hard veneer like rosewood is inclined to break away and is even difficult to cut accurately with the grain.

Curved cuts bring the problems of the cut being partly with and partly against the grain. In difficult cases it helps to put some Sellotape across the veneer before starting to cut.

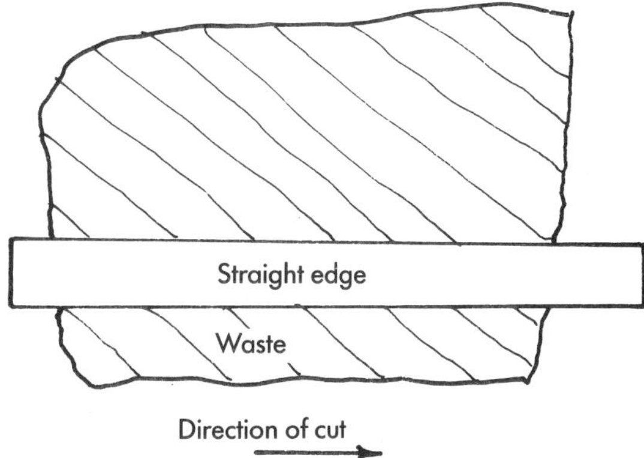

***Figure* 164** *Cutting the veneer*

***Figure* 165** *The tracing in position ready to start the picture*

Tracing

Trace over the simplified drawing. This tracing will be used as a pattern. Choose a piece of flat cheap veneer, large enough to have some spare round the edges, or choose a piece of veneer suitable for the background of the picture. In the example used to illustrate this section a veneer was chosen which was suitable for the sea which forms the picture background. Figure 165 shows the tracing fastened to the top of the veneer.

Window method

There are different ways in which work can proceed, but the one chosen is usually known as the window method. The main outline of the picture is traced onto the backing veneer with carbon paper. One section is then cut out, perhaps the centre strip in the middle of the picture. Choose a suitable veneer and place it under the window which has been cut out. Try various pieces and turn these around to get

***Figure* 166** *Looking at a piece of veneer through a 'window'*

***Figure* 167** *Part way through the marquetry picture*

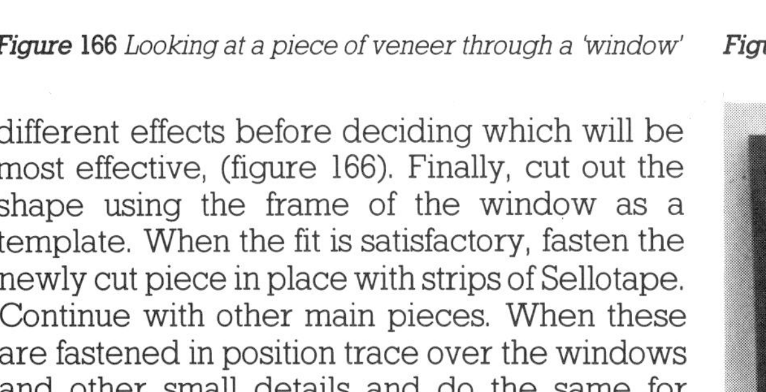

different effects before deciding which will be most effective, (figure 166). Finally, cut out the shape using the frame of the window as a template. When the fit is satisfactory, fasten the newly cut piece in place with strips of Sellotape. Continue with other main pieces. When these are fastened in position trace over the windows and other small details and do the same for these pieces. Figure 167 shows the work in progress. Continue until the picture is complete.

Base

The completed picture needs mounting on a base board. Since this is destined to be a box top, ¼in. (6mm) plywood is suitable. This will give a stable base which will not be liable to move. Select a piece which is free from knots and other defects.

Gluing

PVA glue works admirably in this situation. Apply an even layer of glue to the base and lay the picture on top. Cover with several layers of newspaper to remove any differences in the thicknesses of the various veneers. Place a flat piece of wood over this and cramp them together with 'G' cramps. The newspaper will take care of any glue that may seep through and prevent the cramping wood from sticking to the veneer. Leave it to dry and uncramp.

Counter veneering

Gluing a layer of veneer on one side will tend to warp the base so it is advisable to veneer the other side to restore the balance. Use a veneer which will match the inside of the box.

***Figure* 168** *The completed marquetry picture with a crossbanded border*

Cross banding

The picture will be enhanced if it is given a border. In this example it was decided to use the veneer with the grain running across the width of the strips, which is where the name 'cross' banding comes from. First of all trim round the border of the picture. Now cut the cross banding and mitre the corners. Glue them in place and secure with Sellotape. More than one piece can be butted together to make up the required length if the veneer cannot be cut into strips which are long enough for the sides of the picture.

Cleaning up

To clean up the picture first of all remove any Sellotape. Be very careful removing any large pieces of tape, since it could tear the grain of the veneer if the pull is against the grain. At the slightest sign of this, reverse directions. Glass-

Figure 169 *Parquetry top using sapele veneer*

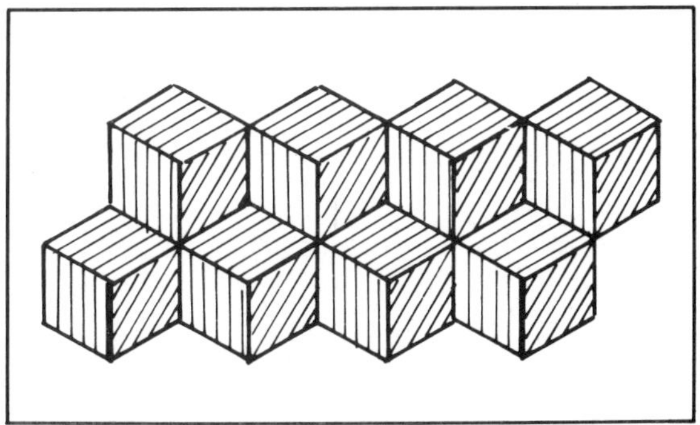

Figure 170 *Alternative parquetry*

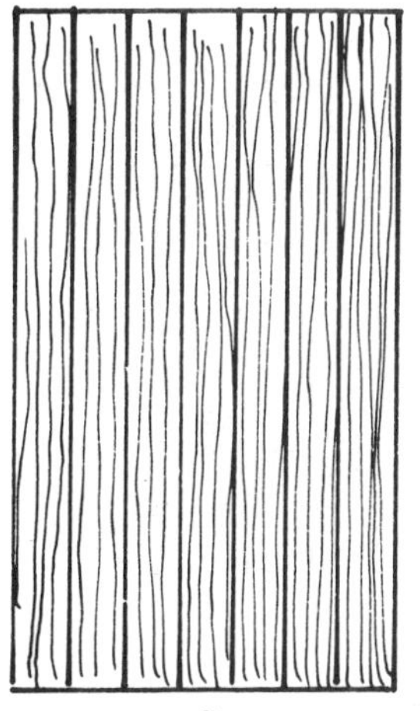

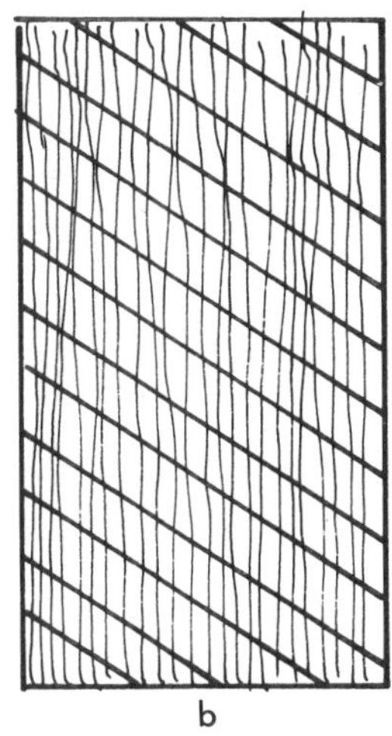

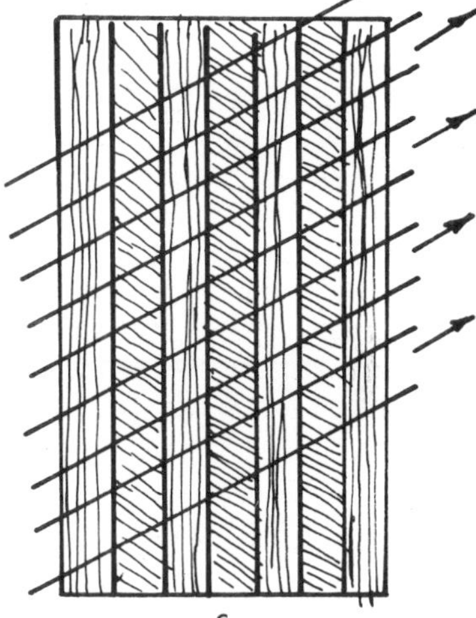

Figure 171 *Parquetry*

paper using a cork block, taking care not to penetrate the veneer. If any small areas have not glued properly then a warm iron can be used to soften the glue and provides a second chance.

Trim the edges of the board if necessary.

Polishing

This is covered in Chapter 14.

The top is now ready to become part of a box. Figure 168 shows this stage.

PARQUETRY

This is another form of decoration using veneer. Here a geometrical design is built up. In figure 169 the design is based on an angle of 60 degrees. (An alternative pattern is shown in figure 170.) Figure 171 shows the stages in the build up.

1 Cut a series of strips 1½in. (38mm) wide and parallel to the grain.
2 Cut a second series also 1½in. (38mm) wide but this time at an angle of 60 degrees to the grain.
3 Tape these strips together alternately.
4 Cut across at 60 degrees making more strips the same width.
5 Move alternate strips one space and tape together.
6 Cut out a square of the required size.
7 Glue on to a suitable base as described under marquetry.

MOTIFS

These are prepared designs which can be bought mounted on stiff paper. Figure 38 shows one such motif.

Settle the motif in the exact position it is to occupy and scribe round it with the point of a sharp knife. Remove the waste to a depth slightly less than the thickness of the motif. Chop lightly across the grain and remove the waste with a chisel. Test the fit and then glue it in with the paper side uppermost. Hold it in place with a 'G' cramp until the glue is dry. Finally, the whole piece can be glasspapered. Figure 42 shows a completed top.

As an alternative, the motif can be taped into a piece of veneer and laid with it.

FURTHER READING

Bairstow, J. *Practical and Decorative Woodworking Joints*, B.T. Batsford Ltd, London

Bennett, M. *Refinishing Antique Furniture*, Dryad Press Ltd, London

Farleigh, J. *Engraving on Wood*, Dryad Press Ltd, London

Gregory, A. *Woodworking*, Dryad Press Ltd, London

Hawkins, D. *Technique of Wood Surface Decoration*, B.T. Batsford Ltd, London

Johnston, D. *Wood Handbook for Craftsmen*, B.T. Batsford Ltd, London

Lincoln, W.A. *The Art and Practice of Marquetry*, Thames & Hudson Ltd, London

Pain, F. *The Practical Woodturner*, Evans Bros Ltd, London

Stokes, G. *Modern Woodturning*, Evans Bros Ltd, London

Trussell, J. *Making Furniture*, Dryad Press Ltd, London

SUPPLIERS

Exotic timbers and laburnum oysters

North Heigham Sawmills
Paddock Street, Norwich NR2 4TW

and most other good sawmills

Veneers, fittings and a useful manual and catalogue

The Art Veneer Company
Industrial Estate, Mildenhall, Suffolk IP28 7AY

Catches, small hinges and locks

W. Hobby Ltd
Knights Hill Square, London SE27 OHH

INDEX